Preface

This anthology contains poems which are with two or three exceptions 'modern'; they are concerned with telling a story, however short. Some poems are confined to a single incident, little more than an anecdote; others deal at length with a series of events, the best example being the only extract (as distinct from a complete poem) in this anthology—the lines from *Reynard the Fox*. This poem is too long for inclusion in this book, but the excerpts form a complete sequence of events.

At one time it used to be a practice to divide poetry, like Gaul, into three parts: lyrical, narrative, and dramatic. Modern verse does not lend itself to such treatment, even if it were desirable. The word 'narrative' seems too dignified to apply to many of the tales and short stories in this book; it might well be argued that some poems are not even stories but are songs or lyrics which have a story element, much in the style of a medieval ballad. Charles Causley obviously has the medieval ballad in mind and the excellence of 'ballad metre' for narrative purposes when writing his 'ballad poems'; the medieval ballads were concerned also with song and dance as well as stories. The long narrative poem has yielded in popularity to the novel and especially the short story, for modern life allows us less and less time to stand and stare. But many story poems by their quality of writing and interest of subject matter deserve at least a favourable comparison with the longer narrative poems of the Victorians.

This collection contains examples of the most popular forms of story-telling in verse—blank verse, rhyming couplets, and stanzas using various schemes, in particular those associated with the medieval ballads. Story poems are written to entertain; the poet has a story, however short, to tell in a manner which he feels will be of interest and pleasure to the reader. It may be a familiar story written from an unusual angle and therefore interesting, or it may be a new story with all the attraction of novelty. But above all the poet wants his readers to share his enjoyment in his story which he hopes will hold children from play and old men from the chimney-corner.

June 1982 F. E .S. F.

Telling Tales

Telling Tales

An anthology of short stories in verse

compiled by F. E. S. Finn

John Murray

Other collections of modern verse by F. E. S. Finn include

Poems of the Sixties
Poets of Our Time
Here and Human
Voices of Today

First published 1982
by John Murray (Publishers) Ltd
50 Albemarle Street
London W1X 4BD

Printed in Great Britain by
Martins Printing Works, Berwick-upon-Tweed

British Library Cataloguing in Publication Data
Telling Tales.
 1. English poetry, 20th century
 I. Finn, F.E.S.
 821'.914'08 PR1225

ISBN 0-7195-3993-5

Contents

THE HAWK

On Sunday the hawk fell on Bigging
  And a chicken screamed
  Lost in its own little snowstorm.
And on Monday he fell on the moor
  And the Field Club
  Raised a hundred silent prisms.
And on Tuesday he fell on the hill
  And the happy lamb
  Never knew why the loud collie straddled him.
And on Wednesday he fell on a bush
  And the blackbird
  Laid by his little flute for the last time.
And on Thursday he fell on Cleat
  And peerie Tom's rabbit
  Swung in a single arc from shore to hill.
And on Friday he fell on a ditch
  But the rampant rat,
  That eye and that tooth, quenched his flame.
And on Saturday he fell on Bigging
  And Jock lowered his gun
  And nailed a small wing over the corn.

George Mackay Brown

THE FISH

I caught a tremendous fish
and held him beside the boat
half out of water, with my hook
fast in a corner of his mouth.
He didn't fight.
He hadn't fought at all.
He hung a grunting weight,
battered and venerable

and homely. Here and there
his brown skin hung in strips
like ancient wallpaper,
and its pattern of darker brown
was like wallpaper;
shapes like full-blown roses
stained and lost through age.
He was speckled with barnacles,
fine rosettes of lime,
and infested
with tiny white sea-lice,
and underneath two or three
rags of green weed hung down.
While his gills were breathing in
the terrible oxygen
— the frightening gills,
fresh and crisp with blood,
that can cut so badly —
I thought of the coarse white flesh
packed in like feathers,
the big bones and the little bones,
the dramatic reds and blacks
of his shiny entrails,
and the pink swim-bladder
like a big peony.
I looked into his eyes
which were far larger than mine
but shallower, and yellowed,
the irises backed and packed
with tarnished tinfoil
seen through the lenses
of old scratched isinglass.
They shifted a little, but not
to return my stare.
— It was more like the tipping
of an object toward the light.
I admired his sullen face,
the mechanism of his jaw,
and then I saw
that from his lower lip
— if you could call it a lip —
grim, wet, and weaponlike,
hung five old pieces of fish-line,
or four and a wire leader

with the swivel still attached,
with all their five big hooks
grown firmly in his mouth.
A green line, frayed at the end
where he broke it, two heavier lines,
and a fine black thread
still crimped from the strain and snap
when it broke and he got away.
Like medals with their ribbons
frayed and wavering,
a five-haired beard of wisdom
trailing from his aching jaw.
I stared and stared
and victory filled up
the little rented boat,
from the pool of bilge
where oil had spread a rainbow
around the rusted engine
to the bailer rusted orange,
the sun-cracked thwarts,
the oarlocks on their strings,
the gunnels — until everything
was rainbow, rainbow, rainbow!
And I let the fish go.

Elizabeth Bishop

From REYNARD THE FOX

From the Gallows Hill to the Tineton Copse
There were ten ploughed fields, like ten full-stops,
All wet red clay, where a horse's foot
Would be swathed, feet thick, like an ash-tree root.
The fox raced on, on the headlands firm,
Where his swift feet scared the coupling worm;
The rooks rose raving to curse him raw,
He snarled a sneer at their swoop and caw.
Then on, then on, down a half-ploughed field
Where a ship-like plough drove glitter-keeled,
With a bay horse near and a white horse leading,
And a man saying 'Zook,' and the red earth bleeding.
He gasped as he saw the ploughman drop
The stilts and swear at the team to stop.

The ploughman ran in his red clay clogs,
Crying 'Zick un, Towzer; zick, good dogs!'
A couple of wire-haired lurchers lean
Arose from his wallet, nosing keen;
With a rushing swoop they were on his track,
Putting chest to stubble to bite his back.
He swerved from his line with the curs at heel,
The teeth as they missed him clicked like steel.
With a worrying snarl, they quartered on him,
While the ploughman shouted, 'Zick; upon him.'

* * * * *

The lurcher dogs soon shot their bolt,
And the fox raced on by the Hazel Holt,
Down the dead grass tilt to the sandstone gash
Of the Pantry Brook at Tineton Ash.
The loitering water, flooded full,
Had yeast on its lip like raddled wool,
It was wrinkled over with Arab script
Of eddies that twisted up and slipped.
The stepping-stones had a rush about them,
So the fox plunged in and swam without them.
He crossed to the cattle's drinking shallow,
Firmed up with rush and the roots of mallow;
He wrung his coat from his draggled bones
And romped away for the Sarsen Stones.
A sneaking glance with his ears flexed back
Made sure that his scent had failed the pack,
For the red clay, good for corn and roses,
Was cold for scent and brought hounds to noses.
He slackened pace by the Tineton Tree
(A vast hollow ash-tree grown in three),
He wriggled a shake and padded slow,
Not sure if the hounds were on or no.
A horn blew faint, then he heard the sounds
Of a cantering huntsman, lifting hounds;
The ploughman had raised his hat for sign,
And the hounds were lifted and on his line.
He heard the splash in the Pantry Brook,
And a man's voice: 'Thiccy's the line he took.'
And a clear 'Yoi doit!' and a whimpering quaver,
Though the lurcher dogs had dulled the savour.
The fox went off while the hounds made halt,
And the horses breathed and the field found fault,

But the whimpering rose to a crying crash
By the hollow ruin of Tineton Ash.
Then again the kettledrum horsehooves beat,
And the green blades bent to the fox's feet,
And the cry rose keen not far behind
Of the 'Blood, blood, blood,' in the foxhounds' mind.

* * * * *

The fox was strong, he was full of running,
He could run for an hour and then be cunning,
But the cry behind him made him chill,
They were nearer now and they meant to kill.
They meant to run him until his blood
Clogged on his heart as his brush with mud,
Till his back bent up and his tongue hung flagging,
And his belly and brush were filthed from dragging.
Till he crouched stone-still, dead-beat and dirty,
With nothing but teeth against the thirty.
And all the way to that blinding end
He would meet with men and have none his friend:
Men to holloa and men to run him,
With stones to stagger and yells to stun him;
Men to head him, with whips to beat him,
Teeth to mangle and mouths to eat him.
And all the way, that wild high crying.
To cold his blood with the thought of dying,
The horn and the cheer, and the drum like thunder
Of the horsehooves stamping the meadows under.
He upped his brush and went with a will
For the Sarsen Stones on Wan Dyke Hill.

* * * * *

Past Tineton Church, over Tineton Waste,
With the lolloping ease of a fox's haste,
The fur on his chest blown dry with the air,
His brush still up and his cheek-teeth bare.
Over the Waste, where the ganders grazed,
The long swift lilt of his loping lazed,
His ears cocked up as his blood ran higher,
He saw his point, and his eyes took fire.
The Wan dyke Hill with its fir-tree barren,
Its dark of gorse and its rabbit-warren,
The Dyke on its heave like a tightened girth,
And holes in the Dyke where a fox might earth.

He had rabbited there long months before,
The earths were deep and his need was sore;
The way was new, but he took a bearing,
And rushed like a blown ship billow-sharing.

* * * * *

The fox raced on, up the Barton Balks,
With a crackle of kex in the nettle stalks,
Over Hammond's grass to the dark green line
Of the larch-wood smelling of turpentine.
Scratch Steven Larches, black to the sky,
A sadness breathing with one long sigh,
Grey ghosts of trees under funeral plumes,
A mist of twig over soft brown glooms.
As he entered the wood he heard the smacks,
Chip-jar, of the fir-pole feller's axe.
He swerved to the left to a broad green ride,
Where a boy made him rush for the farther side.
He swerved to the left, to the Barton Road,
But there were the timberers come to load—
Two timber-carts and a couple of carters
With straps round their knees instead of garters.
He swerved to the right, straight down the wood,
The carters watched him, the boy hallooed.
He leaped from the larch-wood into tillage,
The cobbler's garden of Barton village.

* * * * *

The fox swerved left and scrambled out,
Knocking crinked green shells from the brussels-sprout
He scrambled out through the cobbler's paling,
And up Pill's orchard to Purton's Tailing,
Across the plough at the top of bent,
Through the heaped manure to kill his scent,
Over to Aldam's, up to Cappell's,
Past Nursery Lot with its whitewashed apples,
Past Colston's Broom, past Gaunt's, past Shere's,
Past Foxwhelps' Oasts with their hooded ears,
Past Monk's Ash Clerewell, past Beggars' Oak,
Past the great elms blue with the Hinton smoke.
Along Long Hinton to Hinton Green,
Where the wind-washed steeple stood serene
With its golden bird still sailing air.
Past Banner Barton, past Chipping Bare,

Past Maddings Hollow, down Dundry Dip,
And up Goose Grass to the Sailing Ship.
The three black firs of the Ship stood still
On the bare chalk heave of the Dundry Hill.
The fox looked back as he slackened past
The scaled red-bole of the mizzen-mast.
The moan of the three great firs in the wind
And the 'Ai' of the foxhounds died behind;
Wind-dapples followed the hill-wind's breath
On the Kill Down Gorge where the Danes found death.
Larks scattered up; the peewits feeding
Rose in a flock from the Kill Down Steeding.
The hare leaped up from her form and swerved
Swift left for the Starveall, harebell-turved.
On the wind-bare thorn some longtails prinking
Cried sweet as though wind-blown glass were chinking.
Behind came thudding and loud halloo,
Or a cry from hounds as they came to view.

* * * * *

The pure clean air came sweet to his lungs,
Till he thought foul scorn of those crying tongues.
In a three mile more he would reach the haven
In the Wan Dyke croaked on by the raven.
In a three mile more he would make his berth
On the hard cool floor of a Wan Dyke earth,
Too deep for spade, too curved for terrier,
With the pride of the race to make rest the merrier.
In a three mile more he would reach his dream,
So his game heart gulped and he put on steam.
Like a rocket shot to a ship ashore
The lean red bolt of his body tore,
Like a ripple of wind running swift on grass;
Like a shadow on wheat when a cloud blows past,
Like a turn at the buoy in a cutter sailing
When the bright green gleam lips white at the railing.
Like the April snake whipping back to sheath,
Like the gannets' hurtle on fish beneath,
Like a kestrel chasing, like a sickle reaping,
Like all things swooping, like all things sweeping,
Like a hound for stay, like a stag for swift,
With his shadow beside like spinning drift.
Past the gibbet-stock all stuck with nails,
Where they hanged in chains what had hung at jails,

Past Ashmundshowe where Ashmund sleeps,
And none but the tumbling peewit weeps,
Past Curlew Calling, the gaunt grey corner
Where the curlew comes as a summer mourner,
Past Blowbury Beacon, shaking his fleece,
Where all winds hurry and none brings peace;
Then down on the mile-long green decline,
Where the turf's like spring and the air's like wine,
Where the sweeping spurs of the downland spill
Into Wan Brook Valley and Wan Dyke Hill.

* * * * *

On he went with a galloping rally
Past Maesbury Clump for Wan Brook Valley.
The blood in his veins went romping high,
'Get on, on, on, to the earth or die.'
The air of the downs went purely past
Till he felt the glory of going fast,
Till the terror of death, though there indeed,
Was lulled for a while by his pride of speed.
He was romping away from hounds and hunt,
He had Wan Dyke Hill and his earth in front,
In a one mile more when his point was made
He would rest in safety from dog or spade;
Nose between paws he would hear the shout
Of the 'Gone to earth!' to the hounds without,
The whine of the hounds, and their cat-feet gadding,
Scratching the earth, and their breath pad-padding:
He would hear the horn call hounds away,
And rest in peace till another day.
In one mile more he would lie at rest,
So for one mile more he would go his best.
He reached the dip at the long droop's end
And he took what speed he had still to spend.

So down past Maesbury beech-clump grey
That would not be green till the end of May,
Past Arthur's Table, the white chalk boulder,
Where pasque flowers purple the down's grey shoulder,
Past Quichelm's Keeping, past Harry's Thorn,
To Thirty Acre all thin with corn.
As he raced the corn towards Wan Dyke Brook
The pack had view of the way he took;
Robin hallooed from the downland's crest,

He capped them on till they did their best.
The quarter-mile to the Wan Brook's brink
Was raced as quick as a man can think.

* * * * *

And here, as he ran to the huntsman's yelling,
The fox first felt that the pace was telling;
His body and lungs seemed all grown old,
His legs less certain, his heart less bold,
The hound-noise nearer, the hill-slope steeper,
The thud in the blood of his body deeper.
His pride in his speed, his joy in the race,
Were withered away, for what use was pace?
He had run his best, and the hounds ran better,
Then the going worsened, the earth was wetter.
Then his brush drooped down till it sometimes dragged,
And his fur felt sick and his chest was tagged
With taggles of mud, and his pads seemed lead,
It was well for him he'd an earth ahead.

Down he went to the brook and over,
Out of the corn and into the clover,
Over the slope that the Wan Brook drains,
Past Battle Tump where they earthed the Danes,
Then up the hill that the Wan Dyke rings
Where the Sarsen Stones stand grand like kings.
Seven Sarsens of granite grim,
As he ran them by they looked at him;
As he leaped the lip of their earthen paling
The hounds were gaining and he was failing.
He passed the Sarsens, he left the spur,
He pressed uphill to the blasted fir,
He slipped as he leaped the hedge; he slithered.
'He's mine,' thought Robin. 'He's done; he's dithered.'

* * * * *

At the second attempt he cleared the fence,
He turned half-right where the gorse was dense,
He was leading hounds by a furlong clear.
He was past his best, but his earth was near.
He ran up gorse to the spring of the ramp,
The steep green wall of the dead men's camp,
He sidled up it and scampered down
To the deep green ditch of the Dead Men's Town.

Within, as he reached that soft green turf,
The wind, blowing lonely, moaned like surf,
Desolate ramparts rose up steep
On either side, for the ghosts to keep.
He raced the trench, past the rabbit warren,
Close-grown with moss which the wind made barren;
He passed the spring where the rushes spread,
And there in the stones was his earth ahead.
One last short burst upon failing feet—
There life lay waiting, so sweet, so sweet,
Rest in a darkness, balm for aches.

* * * * *

The earth was stopped. It was barred with stakes.

John Masefield

HUNTING SONG

The fox he came lolloping, lolloping,
Lolloping. His eyes were bright,
His ears were high.
He was like death at the end of a string
When he came to the hollow
Log. He ran in one side
And out of the other. O
He was sly.

The hounds they came tumbling, tumbling,
Tumbling. Their heads were low,
Their eyes were red.
The sound of their breath was louder than death
When they came to the hollow
Log. They boiled at one end
But a bitch found the scent. O
They were mad.

The hunter came galloping, galloping,
Galloping. All damp was his mare
From her hooves to her mane.
His coat and his mouth were redder than death

When he came to the hollow
Log. He took in the rein
And over he went. O
He was fine.

The log he just lay there, alone in
The clearing. No fox nor hound
Nor mounted man
Saw his black round eyes in their perfect disguise
(As the ends of a hollow
Log). He watched death go through him,
Around him and over him. O
He was wise.

Donald Finkel

PIKE

Pike, three inches long, perfect
Pike in all parts, green tigering the gold.
Killers from the egg: the malevolent aged grin.
They dance on the surface among the flies.

Or move, stunned by their own grandeur,
Over a bed of emerald, silhouette
Of submarine delicacy and horror.
A hundred feet long in their world.

In ponds, under the heat-struck lily pads—
Gloom of their stillness:
Logged on last year's black leaves, watching upwards.
Or hung in an amber cavern of weeds

The jaws' hooked clamp and fangs
Not to be changed at this date;
A life subdued to its instrument;
The gills kneading quietly, and the pectorals.

Three we kept behind glass,
Jungled in weed: three inches, four,
And four and a half: fed fry to them—
Suddenly there were two. Finally one

With a sag belly and the grin it was born with.
And indeed they spare nobody.
Two, six pounds each, over two feet long,
High and dry and dead in the willow-herb—

One jammed past its gills down the other's gullet:
The outside eye stared: as a vice locks—
The same iron in this eye
Though its film shrank in death.

A pond I fished, fifty yards across,
Whose lilies and muscular tench
Had outlasted every visible stone
Of the monastery that planted them—

Stilled legendary depth:
It was as deep as England. It held
Pike too immense to stir, so immense and old
That past nightfall I dared not cast

But silently cast and fished
With the hair frozen on my head
For what might move, for what eye might move.
The still splashes on the dark pond,

Owls hushing the floating woods
Frail on my ear against the dream
Darkness beneath night's darkness had freed,
That rose slowly towards me, watching.

Ted Hughes

THE BIRTH OF A SHARK

What had become of the young shark?
It was time for the ocean to move on.
Somehow, sheathed in the warm current
He'd lost his youthful bite, and fell
Shuddering among the feelers of kelp
And dragging weeds. His belly touched sand,
The shark ran aground on his shadow.

Shark-shape, he lay there.
But in the world above
Six white legs dangled, thrashing for the fun of it,
Fifty feet above the newborn shadow.

The shark nosed up to spy them out;
He rose slowly, a long grey feather
Slendering up through the dense air of the sea.
His eyes of bolted glass were fixed
On a roundness of sun and whetted flesh,
Glittering like stars above his small brain—

The shark rose gradually. He was half-grown,
About four feet: strength of a man's thigh
Wrapped in emery, his mouth a watery
Ash of brambles. As he rose
His shadow paled and entered the sand,
Dissolved, in the twinkling shoals of driftsand
Which his thrusting tail spawned.

This was shark's birth in our world.
His grey parents had left him
Mysteriously and rapidly—
How else is a shark born?
They had bequeathed him the odour of blood,
And a sense half of anguish at being
Perpetually the forerunner of blood:
A desire to sleep in the currents fought
Against the strong enchanting links of hunger,
In shoals or alone,
Cruising the white haze off Africa,
Bucked Gibraltar, rode into the Atlantic—
Diet of squid, pulps, a few sea-perch.

But what fish-sense the shark had
Died with his shadow. This commonplace
Of kicking legs he had never seen:
He was attracted. High above him
The sunsoaked heads were unaware of the shark—
He was something rising under their minds
You could not have told them about: grey thought
Beneath the fortnight's seaside spell—
A jagged effort to get at something painful.

He knew the path up was direct:
But the young shark was curious.
He dawdled awhile, circling like a bee
Above stems, cutting this new smell
From the water in shapes of fresh razors.
He wasn't even aware he would strike;
That triggered last thrust was beyond his edgy
Power to choose or predict. This
Was carefully to be savoured first, as later
He'd get it, with expertise, and hit fast.

He knew he was alone.
He knew he could only snap off
A foot or a hand at a time—
And without fuss—for sharks and dogs
Do not like to share.
The taste for killing was not even pleasure to him.
And this was new:
This was not sea-flesh, but a kind
Of smoky scent of suntan oil and salt,
Hot blood and wet cloth. When he struck at it
He only grazed his snout,
And skulked away like a pickpocket—

Swerved, paused, turned on his side,
And cocked a round eye up at the dense
Thrashings of frightened spray his climb touched.

And the thrashing commotion moved
Fast as fire away, on the surface of sun.
The shark lay puzzling
In the calm water ten feet down,
As the top of his eye exploded above
Reef and sand, heading for the shallows.
Here was his time of choice—
Twisting, he thought himself round and round
In a slow circling of doubt,
Powerless to be shark, a spawned insult.

But while he was thinking, the sea ahead of him
Suddenly reddened; and black
Shapes with snouts of blunted knives
Swarmed past him and struck
At the bladder of sunlight, snapping at it.

The shark was blinded—
His vision came to him,
Shred by piece, bone by bone
And fragments of bone. Instinctively
His jaws widened to take these crumbs
Of blood from the bigger, experienced jaws,
Whose aim lay in their twice-his-length
Trust in the body and shadow as one
Mouthful of mastery, speed, and blood—

He learned this, when they came for him;
The young shark found his shadow again.
He learned his place among the weeds.

David Wevill

SHEEP KILLER

I should have known, when I undid his chain,
That darkness had been busy at his brain
As at an anvil, sharpening a fang.
I should have known it by the glint that sprang
Into his eyes when the chain fell and he
Stood stiffly there as though to let me see
That he had all the time in the world to spare,
If I so felt, to match me stare for stare,
His heart being innocent.
I watched him go
Out through the gate with just the faintest show
Of hurry in his trot as though he kept
His body back from where his thoughts leapt
Ahead to the red kill; that holding back
A dog will never show unless the track
He follows is a secret he would keep
From men whose fingers smell of lambs and sheep.

I should have known, had I but had the eye,
That strain in hip and curving flank and thigh;
For what must happen in a hawk's neck when
He spots the quail way down there but with men
Too near in yard or paddock to make safe
The whistling lunge; the tension of that chafe

That is when the lust has the red tongue on fire
But cunning is the muzzle on desire.

So he went slowly till I lost him quite
In the thick fog that made another night
Over the paddocks where beneath the trees
The lambs would be hard at it on their knees
Draining the heavy udders. In that fog
A lamb would learn the coming of a dog
Too late even to get upon its feet
Or in one wild and lost and desperate bleat
To say that death was hard and life was sweet.

He got his fifty in a mile that day
Crunched through the shoulders in the killer's way,
Ribs broken in to crush the leaping heart.
Though great my loss, I recognized the art
With which the thing was done. What speed, what power
He must have known for that one breathless hour
When long restraint was straw before the urge
Of instinct, the red longing, the hot surge
That leapt and thundered and would not be still
Till fifty lambs lay dead about the hill.

He always liked to work the sheep close in,
Sniffing the blood, no doubt, beneath the skin
He dared not tear because of watching eyes.
Why did I trust that shifty compromise!
Why must sheep stand, by fear together drifted,
Helpless as flowers when the scythe is lifted!
Who was at fault, the dog, or I, or the sheep?

But since the farmer must needs have his sleep
That night I put a bullet in his head,
Gave the world back to God, and went to bed.

Ernest G. Moll

ABBEY TOMB

I told them not to ring the bells
The night the Vikings came
Out of the sea and passed us by.

The fog was thick as cream
And in the abbey we stood still
As if our breath might blare
Or pulse rattle if we once
Stopped staring at the door.

Through the walls and through the fog
We heard them passing by.
The deafer monks thanked God too soon
And later only I
Could catch the sound of prowling men
Still present in the hills
So everybody else agreed
To ring the abbey bells.

And even while the final clang
Still snored upon the air
And while the ringers joked their way
Down round the spiral stair,
Before the spit of fervent prayer
Had dried into the stone
The raiders came back through the fog
And killed us one by one.

Father Abbot at the altar
Lay back with his knees
Doubled under him, caught napping
In the act of praise.
Brother John lay unresponsive
In the warming room.
The spiders came out for the heat
And then the rats for him.

Under the level of the sheep
Who graze here all the time
We lie now, under tourists' feet
Who in good weather come.
I told them not to ring the bells
But centuries of rain
And blustering have made their tombs
Look just as right as mine.

Patricia Beer

LORD LOVELACE

Lord Lovelace rode home from the wars,
  His wounds were black as ice,
While overhead the winter sun
  Hung out its pale device.

The lance was tattered in his hand,
  Sundered his axe and blade,
And in a bloody coat of war
  Lord Lovelace was arrayed.

And he was sick and he was sore
  But never sad was he,
And whistled bright as any bird
  Upon an April tree.

'Soon, soon,' he cried, 'at Lovelace Hall
  Fair Ellen I shall greet,
And she with loving heart and hand
  Will make my sharp wounds sweet.

'And young Jehan the serving-man
  Will bring the wine and bread,
And with a yellow link will light
  Us to the bridal bed.'

But when he got to Lovelace Hall
  Burned were both wall and stack,
And in the stinking moat the tower
  Had tumbled on its back.

And none welcomed Lord Lovelace home
  Within the castle shell,
And ravaged was the land about
  That Lord Lovelace knew well.

Long in his stirrups Lovelace stood
  Before his broken door,
And slowly rode he down the hill
  Back to the bitter war.

Nor mercy showed he from that day,
  Nor tear fell from his eye,

And rich and poor both fearful were
  When Black Lovelace rode by.

This tale is true that now I tell
  To woman and to man,
As fair Ellen is my wife's name
  And mine is young Jehan.

Charles Causley

'O WHAT IS THAT SOUND?'

O what is that sound which so thrills the ear
  Down in the valley drumming, drumming?
Only the scarlet soldiers, dear,
  The soldiers coming.

O what is that light I see flashing so clear
  Over the distance brightly, brightly?
Only the sun on their weapons, dear,
  As they step lightly.

O what are they doing with all that gear,
  What are they doing this morning, this morning?
Only their usual manœuvres, dear,
  Or perhaps a warning.

O why have they left the road down there,
  Why are they suddenly wheeling, wheeling?
Perhaps a change in their orders, dear.
  Why are you kneeling?

O haven't they stopped for the doctor's care,
  Haven't they reined their horses, their horses?
Why, they are none of them wounded, dear,
  None of these forces.

O is it the parson they want, with white hair,
  Is it the parson, is it, is it?
No, they are passing his gateway, dear,
  Without a visit.

O it must be the farmer who lives so near.
  It must be the farmer so cunning, so cunning?
They have passed the farmyard already, dear,
  And now they are running.

O where are you going? Stay with me here!
  Were the vows you swore deceiving, deceiving?
No, I promised to love you, dear,
  But I must be leaving.

O it's broken the lock and splintered the door,
  O it's the gate where they're turning, turning;
Their boots are heavy on the floor
  And their eyes are burning.

W. H. Auden

SPAIN, 1809

All day we had ridden through scarred, tawny hills.
  At last the cool
Of splashing water. Then two blackened mills,
  A slaughtered mule.

And there, crag-perched, the village—San Pedro—
  We came to burn.
(Two convoys ambushed in the gorge below.
  They had to learn.)

Not a sound. Not a soul. Not a goat left behind.
  They had been wise.
Those death's-head hovels watched us, bleared and blind,
  With holes for eyes.

Down the one street's foul gutter slowly crawled
  Like blood, dark-red,
The wine from goatskins, slashed and hacked, that sprawled
  Like human dead.

From a black heap, like some charred funeral-pyre,
  Curled up, forlorn,
Grey wisps of smoke, where they had fed the fire
  With their last corn.

What hatred in that stillness! Suddenly
  An infant's cry.
Child, mother, bedrid crone—we found the three,
  Too frail to fly.

We searched their very straw—one wineskin there.
  We grinned with thirst,
And yet?—that Spanish hate!—what man would dare
  To taste it first?

Below our Captain called, 'Bring down the wench.'
  We brought her down—
Dark brooding eyes that faced the smiling French
  With sullen frown.

'Señora, we are sent to burn the place.
  Your house I spare.'
Her proud chin nestled on her baby's face,
  Still silent there.

'Cold cheer you leave us!—one poor skin of wine!
  Before we sup,
You will honour us, Señora?' At his sign
  One filled a cup.

Calmly she took and, drinking, coldly smiled;
  We breathed more free.
But grimly our captain watched her—'Now your child.'
  Impassively

She made the small mouth swallow. All was well.
  The street was fired.
And we, by that brave blaze, as twilight fell,
  Sat gaily tired,

Laughing and eating, while the wine went round,
  Carefree, until
A child's scream through the darkness. At the sound
  Our hearts stood still.

Dumbly we glanced in one another's eyes.
  Our thirst was dead.
And in its place once more that grim surmise
  Upreared its head.

One dragged her to the firelight. Ashen-grey,
She hissed—'I knew
Not even the straw where an old woman lay
Was safe from you.

'Now you are paid!' I never loved their wine,
Had tasted none.
I will not tell, under that white moonshine,
What things were done.

Twenty men mad with drink, and rage, and dread,
Frenzied with pain—
That night the quiet millstream dribbled red
With blood of Spain.

Under the moon across the gaunt sierra
I fled alone.
Their balls whizzed wide. But in each tree lurked terror,
In each stone.

Yes, men are brave. (Earth were a happier place,
Were men less so.)
But I remember one pale woman's face
In San Pedro.

F. L. Lucas

THE BALLAD OF BANNERS (1944)

Edward the Third had seven sons
Whose names were like the blaze
That fills the western window rose
On summer's pageant days

In solemn tombs where pilgrims kneel
And frescoed legends fade
Under the organ-thundered vault
Their secret bones are laid

Who once were trumpets Kings could hear
By dark Bohemian streams
That called the English youth to cross
The channel of their dreams

And out of bloody deeds that struck
  The dying feudal shame
In penitence and praise create
  The rainbow ghost of fame.

It is the image shall endure
  To mould the age to come
When all the props are stowed away
  And all the actors dumb

And still the ghost of Edward's reign
  From Crécy and Poitiers
Walked the exultant, wave-blessed land
  In Shakespeare's conquering years.

And still it haunts the heart today
  Though tank and aeroplane
Roar through the wasted realm of France
  Where Louis' knights were slain

Whispering of some magnificance
  Old John of Gaunt might know
How to recapture from his dream
  Six centuries ago.

What if some wind of war should blow
  With equinoctial rage
Out of the throat of time unborn
  And blast our island stage

And the great naves should tumble down
  To sink beneath the sheaves
While all the banners stained and torn
  Were lost like autumn leaves

With every painted page that told
  Of famous enterprise
And songs that took the longbowmen
  To dazzle Europe's eyes,

Would the long role of deeds that rang
  From Wales to Aquitaine
Somewhere be stored in God's own eye?
  Or would there but remain

The vacant sky that bears no print
  Of mortal destiny
Though the alternate stars were there
  To watch all history?

John Lehmann

MEN IN GREEN

Oh, there were fifteen men in green,
Each with a tommy-gun,
Who leapt into my plane at dawn;
We rose to meet the sun.

We set our course towards the east
And climbed into the day
Till the ribbed jungle underneath
Like a giant fossil lay.

We climbed towards the distant range
Where two white paws of cloud
Clutched at the shoulders of the pass;
The green men laughed aloud.

They did not fear the ape-like cloud
That climbed the mountain crest
And hung from twisted ropes of air
With thunder in their breast.

They did not fear the summer's sun,
In whose hot centre lie
A hundred hissing cannon shells
For the unwatchful eye.

And when on Dobadura's field
We landed, each man raised
His thumb towards the open sky;
But to their right I gazed.

For fifteen men in jungle green
Rose from the kunai grass
And came towards the plane. My men

In silence watched them pass;
It seemed they looked upon themselves
In Time's prophetic glass.

Oh, there were some leaned on a stick
And some on stretchers lay,
But few walked on their own two feet
In the early green of day.

They had not feared the ape-like cloud
That climbed the mountain crest;
They had not feared the summer's sun
With bullets for their breast.

Their eyes were bright, their looks were dull,
Their skin had turned to clay.
Nature had met them in the night
And stalked them in the day.

And I think still of men in green
On the Soputa track
With fifteen spitting tommy-guns
To keep a jungle back.

David Campbell

CARENTAN O CARENTAN

Trees in the old days used to stand
And shape a shady lane
Where lovers wandered hand in hand
Who came from Carentan.

This was the shining green canal
Where we came two by two
Walking at combat-interval.
Such trees we never knew.

The day was early June, the ground
Was soft and bright with dew.
Far away the guns did sound,
But here the sky was blue.

The sky was blue, but there a smoke
Hung still above the sea
Where the ships together spoke
To towns we could not see.

Could you have seen us through a glass
You would have said a walk
Of farmers out to turn the grass,
Each with his own hay-fork.

The watchers in their leopard suits
Waited till it was time,
And aimed between the belt and boot
And let the barrel climb.

I must lie down at once, there is
A hammer at my knee.
And call it death or cowardice,
Don't count again on me.

Everything's all right, Mother,
Everyone gets the same
At one time or another.
It's all in the game.

I never strolled, nor ever shall,
Down such a leafy lane,
I never drank in a canal,
Nor ever shall again.

There is a whistling in the leaves
And it is not the wind,
The twigs are falling from the knives
That cut men to the ground.

Tell me, Master-Sergeant,
The way to turn and shoot.
But the Sergeant's silent
That taught me how to do it.

O Captain, show us quickly
Our place upon the map.
But the Captain's sickly
And taking a long nap.

Lieutenant, what's my duty,
My place in the platoon?
He too's a sleeping beauty,
Charmed by that strange tune.

Carentan O Carentan
Before we met with you
We never yet had lost a man
Or known what death could do.

Louis Simpson

THE DESERT

Beside the dune high as a tree
  But spreading no tree's shade
A man and boy sat silently
  Working at their trade.

A heap of bones lay on the sand
  Like barkless staves of wood;
And near it lay a second heap
  Polished with thickening blood.

One bone, two bones, three bones were
  Chosen by the man
Who made of them a heart's shape, wide
  As his two hands would span.

The man and boy sat hour by hour
  Calmly, coolly, dumb,
Feeling the scarlet heat as though
  Their blackened skins were numb.

A third heap soon rose at their side
  Like boughs laid for a pyre:
The boy's hand went to it and took
  From many lyres one lyre.

It was a lyre in shape, but where
  The stream of music springs
The lyre was nought, a mouth crying
  Wordlessly for strings.

The boy reached to the heap that shone
  Untouched on the sand
And from its bloody muteness took
  A bloody speaking hand.

He fixed the voice in place, then more,
  And soon the lyre was strung—
A frame made of three human bones,
  Each string a human tongue.

The old man took the brilliant lyre
  And struck its cords of red;
The boy rapt by his side stood up
  As a snake rears up its head

And with no smile and with no sigh
  Moved to the lyre's sounds
In a world all dust save for a man,
  A dancer, and three mounds.

Clifford Dyment

BEDTIME STORY

Long long ago when the world was a wild place
Planted with bushes and peopled by apes, our
Mission Brigade was at work in the jungle.
  Hard by the Congo

Once, when a foraging detail was active
Scouting for green-fly, it came on a grey man, the
Last living man, in the branch of a baobab
  Stalking a monkey.

Earlier men had disposed of, for pleasure,
Creatures whose names we scarcely remember—
Zebra, rhinoceros, elephants, wart-hog,
  Lion, rats, deer. But

After the wars had extinguished the cities
Only the wild ones were left, half-naked
Near the Equator: and here was the last one,
  Starved for a monkey.

By then the Mission Brigade had encountered
Hundreds of such men: and their procedure,
History tells us, was only to feed them;
  Find them and feed them;

Those were the orders. And this was the last one.
Nobody knew that he was, but he was. Mud
Caked on his flat grey flanks. He was crouched, half-
  armed with a shaved spear

Glinting beneath broad leaves. When their jaws cut
Swathes through the bark and he saw fine teeth shine,
Round eyes roll round and forked arms waver
  Huge as the rough trunks

Over his head, he was frightened. Our workers
Marched through the Congo before he was born, but
This was the first time perhaps that he'd seen one.
  Staring in hot still

Silence, he crouched there: then jumped. With a long swing
Down from his branch, he had angled his spear too
Quickly, before they could hold him, and hurled it
  Hard at the soldier

Leading the detail. How could he know Queen's
Orders were only to help him? The soldier
Winced when the tipped spear pricked him. Unsheathing his
  Sting was a reflex.

Later the Queen was informed. There were no more
Men. An impetuous soldier had killed off,
Purely by chance, the penultimate primate.
  When she was certain,

Squadrons of workers were fanned through the Congo
Detailed to bring back the man's picked bones to be
Sealed in the archives in amber. I'm quite sure
  Nobody found them

After the most industrious search, though.
Where had the bones gone? Over the earth, dear,
Ground by the teeth of the termites, blown by the
  Wind, like the dodo's.

George MacBeth

MILLER'S END

When we moved to Miller's End,
  Every afternoon at four
A thin shadow of a shade
  Quavered through the garden-door.

Dressed in black from top to toe
  And a veil about her head
To us all it seemed as though
  She came walking from the dead.

With a basket on her arm
  Through the hedge-gap she would pass,
Never a mark that we could spy
  On the flagstones or the grass.

When we told the garden-boy
  How we saw the phantom glide,
With a grin his face was bright
  As the pool he stood beside.

'That's no ghost-walk,' Billy said,
  'Nor a ghost you fear to stop—
Only old Miss Wickerby
  On a short cut to the shop.'

So next day we lay in wait,
  Passed a civil time of day,
Said how pleased we were she came
  Daily down our garden-way.

Suddenly her cheek it paled,
  Turned, as quick, from ice to flame.
'Tell me,' said Miss Wickerby.
  'Who spoke of me, and my name?'

'Bill the garden-boy.'
                She sighed,
  Said, 'Of course, you could not know
How he drowned—that very pool—
  A frozen winter—long ago.'

Charles Causley

CHURCH SCHOOL

The graves pressed to the windows. At
  My elbow I could see
The tombstones of old parish clerks
  Stood staring in on me;

Gaunt leaning shapes of churchwardens,
  And sextons, row by row;
And back of them the village dead
  A-crowding on tiptoe.

I gave them little heed. Was none
  Disturbed my thinking save
For that which fronted me all day—
  A small forsaken grave

That clutched a rosy spindle tree,
  And else was laid alone;
Railed in till none could pluck a weed
  Or cleanse the bitten stone;

The sleeping place a hundred years,
  Of one Joanna Wilde;
'Eight summers . . .' spoke the crumbling lines,
  'Good scholar, gentle child . . .'

No more. The mosses ate the rest.
  But times when all was still
I thought upon Joanna Wilde,
  And pondered her until

She all but stood before me in
  Her sober woollen dress,
Her pinafore drawn straight and starched
  About her littleness;

Until I knew her braided hair,
  The solemn-lidded look
Turned on her ciphering; the way
  She held her spelling book;

Until it seemed that I could touch
  The diligent small hands

That stitched unending calicoes
  And timeless linen bands;

And that a word of praise would bring
  A colour to her cheek,
And she would smile, a brief shy smile,
  And lift her head and speak,

And tell me if she heard the bell,
  And if she grieved to be
So long away from school. . . . But here
  My sense took hold of me

And I would thrust off foolishness,
  And rise and dim the light,
And leave the desks and tombstones to
  The darkness and the night.

One afternoon the mist came down;
  We scarce could see the wall;
The windows blacked; there was no sky
  Nor any graves at all.

I drew my children to the fire,
  And warm they sat and gay;
But—oh—it seemed a bitter thing
  To lie outside that day;

And all at once I heard my heart
  Run crying sharp and thin,
As like as not her mother called,
  'Joanna, child, come in!'

Should the door have swung? The door
  Stayed on its latch, and fast;
No soft wet footprints tracked the floor;
  No shivering air slid past.

No sounds were there but living sounds;
  The crack of burning wood;
And presently my level voice
  Telling them Red Riding Hood.

But—two full days the darkness held;
  Two mornings by my chair

We found bright spindle sprays, and none
  Could tell who laid them there.

The third day—and the light came back;
  The graves showed washed and green;
The robins sang, and all things were
  As ever they had been;

Except the broken spindle tree,
  Its branches bare and blind;
And something sitting quiet in
  A corner of my mind.

I do not shun Joanna's grave.
  I have no fear of her.
But when the morning comes with mist
  I take the register

And call the fifty names with haste,
  And mark them and have done;
Nor count the heads, lest once again
  There should be fifty-one.

Ada Jackson

NELSON GARDENS

As I was walking in Nelson Gardens
A stroppy young seaman came my way,
He put his candid hand in mine
And these were the words I heard him say:

  Come with me where the winking waters
  Beam as bright as washing-day,
  And Old Man Neptune's darling daughters
  Round their father's garden play.

  Buckle your belt with a Lincoln dollar,
  Turn your money and make a wish,
  The world will touch your lucky collar,
  Jump in your pocket like a flying-fish.

Come with me where the briny billow
Is sweet as the grass upon the hill,
The sun will smooth your single pillow
And the terrible tongue of the clock is still.

Off I went with the easy sailor,
But the truth was hard as stone:
Though we sail the seas together
Each of us must sail alone.

Bitter was the brilliant water,
Ever faster spoke the clock,
And the palace was a prison,
And the pillow was a rock.

Early in the morning when the sun was rising
Up came the moon all rosy-red,
Blew the stars out of the heaven,
Spiked the sky on our mast-head.

By my side I saw my comrade
Freezing in the noonday heat,
And his suit was made of canvas
A lump of lead was at his feet.

Now my hair is white as paper,
Thin my finger as the pen,
As the weather from the winter
Turns to summer once again.

As I was walking in Nelson Gardens
A stroppy young seaman came my way,
He put his candid hand in mine
And those were the words I heard him say.

Charles Causley

THE PARKLANDS

Through the Parklands, through the Parklands
Of the wild and misty north,
Walked a babe of seven summers
In a maze of infant wrath.

And I wondered and I murmured
And I stayed his restless pace
With a courteous eye I held him
In that unfrequented place.

Questioning I drew him to me
Touched him not but with an eye
Full of awful adult power
Challenged every infant sigh.

'Of what race and of what lineage,'
Questioning I held him there,
'Art thou, boy?' He answered nothing
Only stood in icy stare.

Blue his eyes, his hair a flaxen
White fell gently on the breeze,
White his hair as straw and blue
His eyes as distant summer seas.

Steadfastly I gazed upon him
Gazed upon that infant face
Till the parted lips gave utterance
And he spake in measured pace:

'All abandoned are my father's
Parklands, and my mother's room
Houses but the subtle spider
Busy at her spinning loom.

'Dead my father, dead my mother,
Dead their son, their only child.'
'How is this when thou art living
Foolish boy, in wrath beguiled?'

'Ask me not,' he said, and moving
Passed into the distance dim.
High the sun stood in the heavens,
But no shadow followed him.

Stevie Smith

THE GRIESLY WIFE

'Lie still, my newly married wife,
  Lie easy as you can.
You're young and ill accustomed yet
  To sleeping with a man.'

The snow lay thick, the moon was full
  And shone across the floor.
The young wife went with never a word
  Barefooted to the door.

He up and followed sure and fast,
  The moon shone clear and white.
But before his coat was on his back
  His wife was out of sight.

He trod the trail wherever it turned
  By many a mound and scree,
And still the barefoot track led on
  And an angry man was he.

He followed fast, he followed slow,
  And still he called her name,
But only the dingoes of the hills
  Yowled back at him again.

His hair stood up along his neck,
  His angry mind was gone,
For the track of the two bare feet gave out
  And a four-foot track went on.

Her nightgown lay upon the snow
  As it might upon the sheet,
But the track that led on from where it lay
  Was never of human feet.

His heart turned over in his chest,
  He looked from side to side,
And he thought more of his gumwood fire
  Than he did of his griesly bride.

And first he started walking back
  And then began to run

And his quarry wheeled at the end of her track
  And hunted him in turn.

Oh, long the fire may burn for him
  And open stand the door,
And long the bed may wait empty:
  He'll not be back any more.

John Manifold

BALLAD OF JOHN CABLE AND THREE GENTLEMEN

He that had come that morning,
One after the other,
Over seven hills,
Each of a new colour,

Came now by the last tree,
By the red-coloured valley,
To a grey river
Wide as the sea.

There at the shingle
A listing wherry
Awash with dark water;
What should it carry?

There on the shelving,
Three dark gentlemen.
Might they direct him?
Three gentlemen.

'Cable, friend John, John Cable.'
When they saw him they said,
'Come and be company
As far as the far side.'

'Come follow the feet,' they said,
'Of your family,
Of your old father
That came already this way.'

But Cable said, 'First I must go
Once to my sister again;
What will she do come spring
And no man on her garden?

She will say "Weeds are alive
From here to the Stream of Friday;
I grieve for my brother's plowing,"
Then break and cry.'

'Lose no sleep,' they said, 'for that fallow:
She will say before summer,
"I can get me a daylong man,
Do better than a brother." '

Cable said 'I think of my wife:
Dearly she needs consoling;
I must go back for a little
For fear she dies of grieving.'

'Cable,' they said, 'John Cable,
Ask no such wild favour;
Still, if you fear she die soon,
The boat might wait for her.'

But Cable said, 'I remember:
Out of charity let me
Go shore up my poorly mother,
Cries all afternoon.'

They said, 'She is old and far,
Far and rheumy with years,
And, if you like, we shall take
No note of her tears.'

But Cable said, 'I am neither
Your hired man nor maid,
Your dog nor shadow
Nor your ape to be led.'

He said, 'I must go back:
Once I heard someone say
That the hollow Stream of Friday
Is a rank place to lie;

And this word, now I remember,
Makes me sorry: have you
Thought of my own body
I was always good to?

The frame that was my devotion
And my blessing was,
The straight bole whose limbs
Were long as stories —

Now poor thing, left in the dirt
By the Stream of Friday
Might not remember me
Half tenderly.'

They let him nurse no worry;
They said, 'We gave you our word:
Poor thing is made of patience;
Will not say a word.'

'Cable, friend John, John Cable,'
After this they said,
'Come with no company
To the far side.

To a populous place,
A dense city
That shall not be changed
Before much sorrow dry.'

Over shaking water
Toward the feet of his father,
Leaving the hills' colour
And his poorly mother

And his wife at grieving
And his sister's fallow
And his body lying
In the rank hollow,

Now Cable is carried
On the dark river;
Not even a shadow
Followed him over.

On the wide river
Grey as the sea
Flags of white water
Are his company.

W. S. Merwin

THE EXPLOSION

On the day of the explosion
Shadows pointed towards the pithead:
In the sun the slagheap slept.

Down the lane came men in pitboots
Coughing oath-edged talk and pipe-smoke,
Shouldering off the freshened silence.

One chased after rabbits; lost them;
Came back with a nest of lark's eggs;
Showed them; lodged them in the grasses.

So they passed in beards and moleskins,
Fathers, brothers, nicknames, laughter,
Through the tall gates standing open.

At noon, there came a tremor; cows
Stopped chewing for a second; sun,
Scarfed as in a heat-haze, dimmed.

The dead go on before us, they
Are sitting in God's house in comfort,
We shall see them face to face—

Plain as lettering in the chapels
It was said, and for a second
Wives saw men of the explosion

Larger than in life they managed—
Gold as on a coin, or walking
Somehow from the sun towards them,

One showing the eggs unbroken.

Philip Larkin

IN THE SERVANTS' QUARTERS

'Man, you too, aren't you one of these rough followers of the
criminal?
All hanging hereabout to gather how he's going to bear
Examination in the hall.' She flung disdainful glances on
The shabby figure standing at the fire with others there,
Who warmed them by its flare.

'No indeed, my skipping maiden: I know nothing of the trial
here,
Or criminal, if so he be.—I chanced to come this way,
And the fire shone out into the dawn, and morning airs are cold
now;
I, too, was drawn in part by charms I see before me play,
That I see not every day.'

'Ha, ha!' then laughed the constables who also stood to warm
themselves,
The while another maiden scrutinized his features hard,
As the blaze threw into contrast every line and knot that wrinkled
them,
Exclaiming, 'Why, last night when he was brought in by the
guard,
You were with him in the yard!'

'Nay, nay, you teasing wench, I say! You know you speak
mistakenly.
Cannot a tired pedestrian who has legged it long and far
Here on his way from northern parts, engrossed in humble
marketings,
Come in and rest awhile, although judicial doings are
Afoot by morning star?'

'O, come, come!' laughed the constables. 'Why, man, you speak
the dialect
He uses in his answers; you can hear him up the stairs.
So own it. We sha'n't hurt ye. There he's speaking now! His
syllables
Are those you sound yourself when you are talking unawares,
As this pretty girl declares.'

'And you shudder when his chain clinks!' she rejoined. 'O yes, I
noticed it.

And you winced, too, when those cuffs they gave him echoed to
us here.
They'll soon be coming down, and you may then have to defend
yourself
Unless you hold your tongue, or go away and keep you clear
When he's led to judgement near!'

'No! I'll be damned in hell if I know anything about the man!
No single thing about him more than everybody knows!
Must not I even warm my hands but I am charged with
blasphemies?' . . .
—His face convulses as the morning cock that moment crows,
And he droops, and turns, and goes.

Thomas Hardy

CHARLEY LEE

A low moon shone on the desert land and the sage was silver white,
As Lee—a thong round hand and hand—stood straight in the
lantern light.
'You have strung up Red and Burke,' said he,
'And you say that the next will be Charley Lee,
But there's never a rope was made for me.'
And he laughed in the quiet night.

They shaped the noose and they flicked the rope and over the limb it
fell,
And Charley Lee saw the ghost of hope go glimmering down to hell.
Two shadows swung from the cottonwood tree,
And the wind went whispering, 'Charley Lee,'
For the turning shadows would soon be three,
And never a stone to tell.

'Have ye more to say for yourself?' said Gray, 'a message the like, or
prayer?
If ye have, then hasten and have your say. We trailed and we
trapped ye fair,
With fire and iron at Hidden Sink,
Where none but the stolen horses drink,
And the chain but wanted a final link.
Ye were riding my red roan mare.'

'But prove your property first,' said Lee. 'Would you call the mare your own,
With never a brand or mark to see, or name to the big red roan?
But strip the saddle and turn her loose,
And I'll show that the mare is my own cayuse.
And I don't—then take it a fair excuse,
To tighten the rope you've thrown.'

Gaunt, grim faces and steady eyes were touched with a sombre look,
And hands slipped slowly to belted thighs and held on a finger-crook,
For Gray of Mesa who claimed the mare,
Had talked too much as he led them there,
Nor other among them knew the lair,
So a grip on their haste they took.

'Give him a chance,' said Monty Wade, and, 'What is the use?' said Blake.
'He's done,' said Harney; 'his string is played. But we'll give him an even break.'
So they led the mare to the cottonwood tree,
Nor saddle nor bridle nor rope had she,
'Bonnie, come here!' said Charley Lee,
And soft was the word he spake.

The roan mare came and she nosed his side and nuzzled him friendly-wise;
'Kneel!' cried Lee, and he leaped astride and fled as the swallow flies.
Flashes followed his flight in vain,
Bullets spattered the ground like rain,
Hoofs drummed far on the midnight plain,
And a low moon rode the skies.

Dawn broke red on the desert land where the turning shadows fell,
And the wind drove over the rolling sand with a whimpering ebb and swell,
Whimpering, whispering, 'Charley Lee,'
As south on the red roan mare rode he,
Yet the turning shadows they were three,
And never a stone to tell.

Henry Herbert Knibbs

CORONER'S JURY

He was the doctor up to Combe,
Quiet-spoke, dark, weared a moustache,
And one night his wife's mother died
After her meal, and he was tried
                    For poisoning her.

Evidence come up dark's a bag,
But onions is like arsenic:
'Twas eating they, his lawyer said,
And rabbit, 'fore she went to bed,
                    That took her off.

Jury withdrew. 'He saved my child,'
Says 'Lias Lee. 'Think to his wife,'
Says one. 'I tell 'ee, a nit's life
That there old 'ooman led 'em both—
                    Tedious old toad.'

'Give en six months,' says easy Joe.
'You can't do that, sirs,' foreman said,
''Tis neck or nothing, yes or no.'
'All right then, sir,' says Joe. ''Tis no,
                    Not guilty, sir.'

'You, Jabez Halls?' 'I brings it in
Rabbit and onions; that's my thought.
If that didn' kill her, sirs, it ought,
To her age.' So us brought it in
                    Rabbit and onions.

Doctor went free, but missis died
Soon afterward, she broke her heart.
Still Doctor bide on twenty year
Walking the moors, keeping apart
                    And quiet, like.

L. A. G. Strong

SUNSTRIKE

A solitary prospector
staggered, locked in a vision
of slate hills that capered
on the molten horizon.

Waterless, he came to where
a river had run, now a band
flowing only in ripples
of white unquenchable sand.

Cursing, he dug sporadically
here, here, as deep as his arm,
and sat quite still, eyes thirstily
incredulous on his palm.

A handful of alluvial
diamonds leered back, and more: mixed
in the scar, glinted globules
of rubies, emeralds, onyx.

And then he was swimming in fire
and drinking; splashing hot halos
of glittering drops at the choir
of assembled carrion crows.

Douglas Livingstone

THE DAY WE FOUND THE SNOW PALACE

The day that five of us climbed up the gulley
(Five strangers, almost, knowing first names only)
Leaving the others in the sociable valley,
We found a palace of snow.

First the waterfall, smoking and disappearing;
Then this vast tunnel of marble, its chipped sides gleaming
In the scattering sun; then the roar came into hearing.
Marble? No, it was snow.
Snow in July? We clambered down. We leapt

On the hard roof, foamy with mud. Feet slipped
('Is it safe?'). Then we leaned and spat over the abrupt
And scalloped edge of snow.

We waded under the dripping roof ('It's wet!');
Tried it with echoes, pebbles, cameras; sat
Half wanting to see it collapse, as it well might
('This time of year, with snow').

We stayed for hours, fondling the smooth wet rock,
Took snaps of each other, dislodged an enormous log,
Planned what to say to the others when we got back—
'We found a palace of snow,

You should have come—my, but you missed a treat!'
Enjoying our pity, taking belated fright
('If it had fallen in!'), boring the others all night,
Talking of nothing but snow.

All night as I lay in bed the ceiling dripped,
The water spun and sparkled as I half slept,
I could feel a crunch and slither under my feet,
Climbing soft cliffs of snow.

The fears we had boasted came true; the roof collapsed
Crackling and snarling on me, as the others watched.
Someone slipped on the grass and screamed as he splashed,
Vanishing under the snow.

* * *

Now we are home and have parted, the five of us who
In the sudden intimate clutch of discovery saw
That echoing tunnel under the summer snow.

I've forgotten what they looked like by now, those four.
Only now and then I remember the drip and the roar
And wonder idly if the tunnel's still there,

Or whether any of them calls out and wakes,
Hearing the snarl and laugh as the roof creaks
Under the strength of the August sun, and breaks,

Feeling the icy coil around his body, spun
And tugged from the slithering rock, alone, alone,
No friend or lover sobbing or looking on,

Only four intimate strangers with Christian names,
Each calling incomprehensibly as he drowns.

Laurence Lerner

'ANYONE LIVED IN A PRETTY HOW TOWN'

anyone lived in a pretty how town
(with up so floating many bells down)
spring summer autumn winter
he sang his didn't he danced his did.

Women and men(both little and small)
cared for anyone not at all
they sowed their isn't they reaped their same
sun moon stars rain

children guessed(but only a few
and down they forgot as up they grew
autumn winter spring summer)
that noone loved him more by more

when by now and tree by leaf
she laughed his joy she cried his grief
bird by snow and stir by still
anyone's any was all to her

someones married their everyones
laughed their cryings and did their dance
(sleep wake hope and then)they
said their nevers they slept their dream

stars rain sun moon
(and only the snow can begin to explain
how children are apt to forget to remember
with up so floating many bells down)

one day anyone died i guess
(and noone stooped to kiss his face)
busy folk buried them side by side
little by little and was by was

all by all and deep by deep
and more by more they dream their sleep
noone and anyone earth by april
wish by spirit and if by yes.

Women and men(both dong and ding)
summer autumn winter spring
reaped their sowing and went their came
sun moon stars rain

E. E. Cummings

MR GEDGE

Mr Gedge, the retired
Cobbler having many years
Put away last and hammer,
At last found himself

Nailed. Through sixty creased
And down-at-heel years
Eyed with gimlet, plugged with tallow,
He purged the desert of his bench

In a spreading oasis
Of books. Overspilling bookcases,
Their vivid jackets scaled
The walls or lay in piles

Like casualties awaiting
Burial. This, then,
Was his sanctuary. Chrysanthemum,
Rose, gentian—the colours

Vegetated around a hothouse
Of rare editions. He had also
Acquired old manuscripts, sepia maps,
Copper engravings,

Other collectors had got wind of
And coveted. Week in,
Week out, through sixty years
His shadow on the bookstalls bloomed—

Lunettes and elastic-sided
Boots an antiquary's dream. In the end
It got so that he took
To crawling

Between and over *Decline and Fall,*
Enc. Brit. and *B.O.P.*,
And badgered his way out
At night. Under the deadweight

Of so many volumes the floor began
To sag; and dragging
On the walls, cracked them
Like the Tower of Babel.

The Council duly sent along
The Sanitary Inspector (who had never
Read a book in his life). And he
Condemned the whole structure.

Mr Gedge was thereupon
Removed to a council flat. His books
Were uprooted and carted away for disposal
In two hundred very pregnant

Sacks. Auctioneers creaked
Like catalogues as their shark eyes snap-
Snapped. Their kid palms grew callouses
From gavels going-gone as quick as

Cobblers' hammers. Relieved
Of his voluminous burdens of empire,
Mr Gedge rules in an exile of silences
Which are now collecting him.

Roy Bennett

'BUTCH' WELDY

After I got religion and steadied down
They gave me a job in the canning works,
And every morning I had to fill
The tank in the yard with gasoline,

That fed the blow-fires in the sheds
To heat the soldering irons.
And I mounted a rickety ladder to do it,
Carrying buckets full of the stuff.
One morning, as I stood there pouring,
The air grew still and seemed to heave,
And I shot up as the tank exploded,
And down I came with both legs broken,
And my eyes burned crisp as a couple of eggs
For someone left a blow-fire going,
And something sucked the flame in the tank.
The Circuit Judge said whoever did it
Was a fellow-servant of mine, and so
Old Rhodes' son didn't have to pay me.
And I sat on the witness stand as blind
As Jack the Fiddler, saying over and over,
'I didn't know him at all.'

Edgar Lee Masters

OUR BROTHER RICHARD

He went his own rake-helly way;
He gamed and diced and swore.
Bred up in fear and godliness,
He loved the tavern more.

Our father drove him from the house;
We never spoke his name;
But all his trespass was our cross,
His ill-report our shame.

And if we saw him in the street,
We turned our heads aside;
And so it passed, until in rags
And poverty he died.

In life he could be none of ours;
But right is ever right.
He's buried with the family,
His faults turfed out of sight.

His grave is neat as any there;
On Saturdays we go
With roses in the summer-time,
And holly wreaths in snow.

And every Sunday praise the Lord
With calm and thankful brow,
That tidied and respectable,
We can own Richard now.

Ada Jackson

MY FRIEND TOM

My friend Tom's a bit of a laugh:
  There's a motorbike in his smile—
A rod that'll do a ton-and-a-half
  Over the Murder Mile.

My friend Tom's got an iron grip
  On the iron he rides through time:
When he runs people down his wheels hardly slip
  In the slosh of their mashed-up slime.

Cats that grin in the catseyed dark
  Die in a cushioned squeal,
While the dogs that chase them halve their bark,
  Sliced in two by the wheel.

My friend Tom's a skin for the girls
  They clench their knees on his seat
And burp up their beer on his sick leather gear
  While he blows like a gale down the street.

They like the tang of time on their face
  And the blood that shoots up their skirt,
Though some that have ridden behind him
  Lie ahead of him under the dirt:

Daff went straight at a corner,
  Dot carried on from a flips,
And on and then on through some railings
  In neat little vertical strips.

My friend Tom's a bit of a lad,
   And he's bit off a bit of his smile;
The rest of it's spread round the back of his head
   Which is spread round the Murder Mile.

Michael Baldwin

THE BALLAD OF BILLY ROSE

Outside Bristol Rovers' Football Ground—
The date has gone from me, but not the day,
Nor how the dissenting flags in stiff array
Struck bravely out against the sky's grey round—

Near the Car Park then, past Austin and Ford,
Lagonda, Bentley, and a colourful patch
Of country coaches come in for the match,
Was where I walked, having travelled the road

From Fishponds to watch Portsmouth in the Cup,
The Third Round, I believe. And I was filled
With the old excitement which had thrilled
Me so completely when, while growing up,

I went on Saturdays to match or fight.
Not only me; for thousands of us there
Strode forward eagerly, each man aware
Of tingling memory, anticipating delight.

We all marched forward, all, except one man.
I saw him because he was paradoxically still,
A stone against the flood, face upright against us all,
Head bare, hoarse voice aloft, blind as a stone.

I knew him at once, despite his pathetic clothes;
Something in his stance, or his sturdy frame
Perhaps. I could even remember his name
Before I saw it on his blind-man's tray. Billy Rose.

And twenty forgetful years fell away at the sight.
Bare-kneed, dismayed, memory fled to the hub
Of Saturday violence, with friends to the Labour Club,
Watching the boxing on a sawdust summer night.

The boys' enclosure close to the shabby ring
Was where we stood, clenched in a resin world,
Spoke in cool voices, lounged, were artificially bored
During minor bouts. We paid threepence to go in.

Billy Rose fought there. He was top of the bill.
So brisk a fighter, so gallant, so precise!
Trim as a tree he stood for the ceremonies,
Then turned to meet George Morgan of Tirphil.

He had no chance. Courage was not enough,
Nor tight defence. Donald Davies was sick
And we threatened his cowardice with an embarrassed kick.
Ripped across both his eyes was Rose, but we were tough

And clapped him as they wrapped his blindness up
In busy towels, applauded the wave
He gave his executioners, cheered the brave
Blind man as he cleared with a jaunty hop

The top rope. I had forgotten that day
As if it were dead for ever, yet now I saw
Thc flowers of punched blood on the ring floor,
As bright as his name. I do not know

How long I stood with ghosts of the wild fists
And the cries of shaken boys long dead around me,
For struck to act at last, in terror and pity
I threw some frantic money, three treacherous pence—

And I cry at the memory—into his tray, and ran,
Entering the waves of the stadium like a drowning man.
Poor Billy Rose, God, he could fight,
Before my three sharp coins knocked out his sight.

Leslie Norris

SOUVENIRS

Mrs. Stavely-ffoster visited Switzerland.
The cowbells echoed from valley to wooded valley,
The blue-as-gentian air was a carillon:
But all she heard was the castanets of Time
As she bought carved cuckoo clocks and bears and salad servers.

Mrs. Stavely-ffoster felt drawn to Morocco.
Minarets soared skyward from bougainvillea,
Spice-sellers, story-tellers, dancers, snake-charmers
Opened Keats' magic casements on a world of wonder:
But in the souks, flushed and fanatical, she was bargaining
For Berber rugs and a tray of beaten copper.

Mrs. Stavely-ffoster arrived in Venice.
The carved and fretted façades trembled, reflected in water,
Gondolas waited at the Piazza san Marco:
But she (missing the Bridge of Sighs) had found a shop
Selling costly and covetable baubles of blown glass.

Mrs. Stavely-ffoster leant on the ship's rail; across the Tagus
A cock crowed; Lisbon indolently climbing its seven hills
Was a promise of secret alleys, balloon-men, and white peacocks:
But unerringly she sped through the Rossio
In search of a suède coat and a cloth embroidered in Madeira.

Mrs. Stavely-ffoster gave an elegant drinks party
To celebrate her return home to her roses in Sussex.
Look, she cried, look darlings at my souvenirs
That I bought here and there to remind me
Of all the fabulous places I have been visiting.

And her guests, murmuring politely among themselves,
Gazed at her life so precisely displayed on the shelves.

Margaret Rhodes

SADIE AND MAUD

Maud went to college.
Sadie stayed at home.
Sadie scraped life
With a fine-tooth comb.

She didn't leave a tangle in.
Her comb found every strand.
Sadie was one of the livingest chits
In all the land.

Sadie bore two babies
Under her maiden name.
Maud and Ma and Papa
Nearly died of shame.

When Sadie said her last so-long
Her girls struck out from home.
(Sadie had left as heritage
Her fine-tooth comb.)

Maud, who went to college,
Is a thin brown mouse.
She is living all alone
In this old house.

Gwendolyn Brooks

BREDON HILL

In summertime on Bredon
  The bells they sound so clear;
Round both the shires they ring them
  In steeples far and near,
  A happy noise to hear.

Here of a Sunday morning
  My love and I would lie,
And see the coloured counties,
  And hear the larks so high
  About us in the sky.

The bells would ring to call her
  In valleys miles away:
'Come all to church, good people;
  Good people, come and pray.'
  But here my love would stay.

And I would turn and answer
Among the springing thyme,
'Oh, peal upon our wedding,
And we will hear the chime,
And come to church in time.'

But when the snows at Christmas
On Bredon top were strown,
My love rose up so early
And stole out unbeknown
And went to church alone.

They tolled the one bell only,
Groom there was none to see,
The mourners followed after,
And so to church went she,
And would not wait for me.

The bells they sound on Bredon,
And still the steeples hum.
'Come all to church, good people,'—
Oh, noisy bells, be dumb;
I hear you, I will come.

A. E. Housman

IF YOU SHOULD GO TO CAISTOR TOWN

If you should go to Caistor town
Where my true love has gone,
Ask her why she went away
And left me here alone.

She said the Caistor sky was blue,
The wind was never cold,
The pavements were all made of pearl,
The young were never old.

Never a word she told me more
But when the year was fled,
Upon a bed of brightest earth
She laid her gentle head.

When I went up to Caistor
  My suit was made of black,
And all her words like summer birds
  Upon the air came back.

O when I went to Caistor
  With ice the sky was sown,
And all the streets were chill and grey
  And they were made of stone.

Charles Causley

THE JUNIPER TREE

Meet me my love, meet me my love
By the low branching juniper tree
O I will meet you there my love
If no harm come to me
If no harm come to me

Blue burns the cone, blue burns the cone
Of the low branching juniper tree
And there he waited for his love
As the black minutes go by
As the black minutes go by

Bellows in the field a cow, in the field a cow
Bellows loud after its dead calf
As he waited by the juniper tree
And he heard the red fox cough
He heard the red fox cough

Flew through the air, flew through the air an owl
To the low branching juniper tree
As he waited there for his love
And the black minutes went by
And the black minutes went by

The wind blew down, the wind blew down
Into the low branching juniper tree
And all the seeds rattled in the weed
As the wind blew sudden by
As the wind blew sudden by

Then fell the rain, then fell the rain down
Fell cold into black wet sleet
On the low branching juniper tree
And he said why is she late
He said why is she late

I have come to you my love, my love
Waiting by the juniper tree
And he turns to see her standing there
As white as death was she
As white as death was she

Then why are you so long my love, my love
As I waited by the juniper tree?
But now I will kiss your mouth, he said
O never you will, said she
O never you will, said she

Wilfred Watson

THE GOOLE CAPTAIN

One day as I walked by Crocodile Mansions
I met a young woman, sea-green were her eyes,
And she was loud weeping by the banks of the Humber,
O, bitter the sound of her sobs and her sighs.

I asked this young woman why she was sore weeping,
'Pray, tell me,' I said, 'why you grieve by the tide?'
And when I had put my arm tightly around her,
In a voice like a sea bird she sadly replied,

'I was born, sir, at Wetwang, but I left the East Riding,
With the cows and the sheep as a girl I would roam,
And if I were back with my father and brothers
I'd ne'er leave again the sweet fields of my home.'

So I led her gently past Crocodile Mansions,
And I took her so gently by the banks of the Humber,
She gave herself freely, her eyes and her kisses,
And I gave her a gold ring and a necklet of amber.

When we parted at stardown no more was she weeping,
But the very next morning as I sailed out with the tide,
She waved to me gaily as we hove around the headland
And I yearned for her beauty to be by my side.

O, I sailed for a year and a day to the Indies
And I came back to England one green day in spring
But I had forgotten the girl with the green eyes,
The necklet of amber, the little gold ring.

But as I was strolling down the Land of Green Ginger
While our ship loaded up with a cargo for Poole,
The people they looked at me strangely and whispered,
'O, beware of the faithless young captain from Goole.'

So I went off at once to Crocodile Mansions
To look for my dear love with sea-green eyes,
But no-one would tell me or answer my questions,
O, bitter my heart then and empty my sighs.

Then I met in 'The Dragon' a drunken old sailor
Who told me he'd seen her with a necklet of amber,
A little gold ring and her eyes green and staring
Floating far out to sea by the banks of the Humber.

And I walked for the last time by Crocodile Mansions,
My heart was so full I shed never a tear
O, I looked at the sea and I looked at the Humber
And in every green wave were the eyes of my dear.

Leonard Clark

THE BALLAD OF CHARLOTTE DYMOND

Charlotte Dymond, a domestic servant aged eighteen, was murdered near Rowtor Ford on Bodmin Moor on Sunday, 14th April 1844, by her young man, a crippled farm-hand, Matthew Weeks, aged twenty-two. A stone marks the spot.

It was a Sunday evening
  And in the April rain
That Charlotte went from our house
  And never came home again.

Her shawl of diamond redcloth,
  She wore a yellow gown,
She carried the green gauze handkerchief
  She bought in Bodmin town.

About her throat her necklace
  And in her purse her pay:
The four silver shillings
  She had at Lady Day.

In her purse four shillings
  And in her purse her pride
As she walked out one evening
  Her lover at her side.

Out beyond the marshes
  Where the cattle stand,
With her crippled lover
  Limping at her hand.

Charlotte walked with Matthew
  Through the Sunday mist,
Never saw the razor
  Waiting at his wrist.

Charlotte she was gentle
  But they found her in the flood
Her Sunday beads among the reeds
  Beaming with her blood.

Matthew, where is Charlotte,
  And wherefore has she flown?
For you walked out together
  And now are come alone.

Why do you not answer,
  Stand silent as a tree,
Your Sunday worsted stockings
  All muddied to the knee?

Why do you mend your breast-pleat
  With a rusty needle's thread
And fall with fears and silent tears
  Upon your single bed?

Why do you sit so sadly
  Your face the colour of clay
And with a green gauze handkerchief
  Wipe the sour sweat away?

Has she gone to Blisland
  To seek an easier place,
And is that why your eye won't dry
  And blinds your bleaching face?

'Take me home!' cried Charlotte,
  'I lie here in the pit!
A red rock rests upon my breasts
  And my naked neck is split!'

Her skin was soft as sable,
  Her eyes were wide as day,
Her hair was blacker than the bog
  That licked her life away.

Her cheeks were made of honey,
  Her throat was made of flame
Where all around the razor
  Had written its red name.

As Matthew turned at Plymouth
  About the tilting Hoe,
The cold and cunning Constable
  Up to him did go:

'I've come to take you, Matthew,
  Unto the Magistrate's door.
Come quiet now, you pretty poor boy,
  And you must know what for.'

'She is as pure,' cried Matthew,
  'As is the early dew,
Her only stain it is the pain,
  That round her neck I drew!

'She is as guiltless as the day
  She sprang forth from her mother.
The only sin upon her skin
  Is that she loved another.'

They took him off to Bodmin,
  They pulled the prison bell,
They sent him smartly up to Heaven
  And dropped him down to Hell.

All through the granite kingdom
  And on its travelling airs
Ask which of these two lovers
  The most deserves your prayers.

And your steel heart search, Stranger,
  That you may pause and pray
For lovers who come not to bed
  Upon their wedding day,

But lie upon the moorland
  Where stands the sacred snow
Above the breathing river,
  And the salt sea-winds go.

Charles Causley

A CAUTIONARY TALE

Every addled egg
a birdsnester blows
is one more blood-knot
severed.
          Plenty
were blown, and plenty dropped
from the treetops
in Edgeley Wood last spring
by butterfingered boys.
                    Then
one of the birdsnesters slipped
and fell (a boy named Jones
the papers said)
top-heavy, head-first,
his feet the flight
of an arrow whose head
was his.
          Slipped, fell —

and his young yolk spilled
from its fragile shell
high in the leafless
tree of himself; and Jones
was a lifeless
bundle of bones
and puddle of bloody shadow.

There are fewer
boys, there are far
more birds,
in Edgeley Wood
this spring.

Nigel Lewis

LITTLE BOYS OF TEXAS

The little boys of Texas prance
To swimming places without their pants
And dive in deep to cool their souls
In very dubious swimming-holes.

The checkered rattlesnake hides there,
He does not ever care to share
His water, slimy as can be,
With any Christian company.

The diamond-back whose single bite
Is full of everlasting night
Lurks beside the sunken log
Short-tempered as a love-crossed dog.

The hoop-snake puts her sharp tail in
Her mouth and rolls as fast as sin
To be at the water bright and smart
With murder at her slender heart.

And there the deadly cotton-mouth,
Honey-mannered as the South,
Lies saying, 'You-all sure are sweet!'
And stabs quick death into your feet.

But boys of Texas do not fret
So long's the water there is wet,
They drink in quarts of typhoid fever,
And laugh and yell without a quiver.

They never mind a bitten toe,
These grandsons of the Alamo,
They are as tough as spikes and nails,
These Davy Crocketts with hard tails.

And when they leave the slimy bank,
There they lie, stiff, rank on rank,
Cotton-mouth, rattler, hoop, outspread,
Sadder, wiser, and plumb dead.

R. P. Tristram Coffin

THE UNEXPLODED BOMB

Two householders (semi-detached) once found,
Digging their gardens, a bomb underground—
Half in one's land, half in t'other's, with the fence between.
Neighbours they were, but for years had been
Hardly on speaking terms. Now X unbends
To pass a remark across the creosoted fence:
'Look what I've got! . . . Oh! you've got it too.
Then what, may I ask, are you proposing to do
About this object of yours which menaces my wife,
My kiddies, my property, my whole way of life?'
'Your way of life,' says Y, 'is no credit to humanity.
I don't wish to quarrel; but since you began it, I
Find your wife stuck-up, your children repel me,
And let me remind you that we too have the telly.
This bomb of mine—'
'I don't like your tone!
And I must point out that since I own
More bomb than you, to create any tension
Between us won't pay you.'
'What a strange misapprehension!'
Says the other: 'my portion of bomb is near
Six inches longer than yours. So there!'

'They seem,' the bomb muttered in its clenched and narrow
Sleep, 'to take me for a vegetable marrow.'

'It would give me,' said X, 'the very greatest pleasure
To come across the fence now with my tape-measure—'
'Oh no,' Y answered, 'I'm not having you
Trampling my flowerbeds and peering through
My windows.'

'Oho,' snarled X, 'if that's
Your attitude, I warn you to keep your brats
In future from trespassing upon my land,
Or they'll bitterly regret it.'
'You misunderstand.
My family has no desire to step on
Your soil, and my bomb is a peace-lover's weapon.'

Called a passing angel, 'If you two shout
And fly into tantrums and keep dancing about,
The thing will go off. It is surely permissible
To say that your bomb, though highly fissible,
Is in another sense one and indivisible;
By which I mean—if you'll forgive the phrase,
Gentlemen—the bloody thing works both ways.
So let me put forward a dispassionate proposal:
Both of you ring for a bomb-disposal
Unit, and ask them to remove post-haste
The cause of your dispute.'
X and Y stared aghast
At the angel. 'Remove my bomb?' they sang
In unison both: 'allow a gang
To invade my garden and pull up the fence
Upon which my whole way of life depends?
Only a sentimental idealist
Could moot it. I, thank God, am a realist.'

The angel fled. The bomb turned over
In its sleep and mumbled, 'I shall soon discover,
If X and Y are too daft to unfuse me,
How the Devil intends to use me.'

C. Day Lewis

A TRUE STORY

The valley was drowned, the inhabitants
Properly compensated, decently re-housed.
The dam was opened by Her Majesty the Queen.
It was a popular decision at the time
To leave the stone-built village where it stood,
To leave the church and the church bells.
It would be nice, they said, to hear them
Ringing under the water, the bells
Of the drowned village.

After a few years, men went out in boats
And dynamited the steeple
To silence the bells.

This happened, oddly enough,
In England.

Harri Webb

TELEPHONE CONVERSATION

The price seemed reasonable, location
Indifferent. The landlady swore she lived
Off premises. Nothing remained
But self-confession. 'Madam,' I warned,
'I hate a wasted journey—I am—African.'
Silence. Silenced transmission of
Pressurized good-breeding. Voice, when it came,
Lipstick-coated, long gold-rolled
Cigarette-holder pipped. Caught I was, foully.
'HOW DARK?' . . . I had not misheard . . . 'ARE YOU LIGHT
OR VERY DARK?' Button B. Button A. Stench
Of rancid breath of public-hide-and-speak.
Red booth. Red pillar-box. Red doubled-tiered
Omnibus squelching tar. It *was* real! Shamed
By ill-mannered silence, surrender
Pushed dumbfoundment to beg simplification.
Considerate she was, varying the emphasis—
'ARE YOU DARK? OR VERY LIGHT?' Revelation came.
'You mean—like plain or milk chocolate?'

Her assent was clinical, crushing in its light
Impersonality. Rapidly, wavelength adjusted,
I chose, 'West African sepia'—and as an afterthought,
'Down in my passport.' Silence for spectroscopic
Flight of fancy, till truthfulness clanged her accent
Hard on the mouthpiece. 'WHAT'S THAT?' conceding
'DON'T KNOW WHAT THAT IS.' 'Like brunette.'
'THAT'S DARK, ISN'T IT?' 'Not altogether.
Facially, I am brunette, but madam, you should see
The rest of me. Palm of my hand, soles of my feet
Are a peroxide blond. Friction, caused—
Foolishly, madam—by sitting down, has turned
My bottom raven black—One moment, madam!'—sensing
Her receiver rearing on the thunder clap
About my ears—'Madam,' I pleaded, 'Wouldn't you rather
See for yourself?'

Wole Soyinka

BALLAD OF THE LANDLORD

Landlord, landlord,
My roof has sprung a leak.
Don't you 'member I told you about it
Way last week?

Landlord, landlord,
These steps is broken down.
When you come up yourself
It's a wonder you don't fall down.

Ten Bucks you say I owe you?
Ten Bucks you say is due?
Well, that's Ten Bucks more'n I'll pay you
Till you fix this house up new.

What? You gonna get eviction orders?
You gonna cut off my heat?
You gonna take my furniture and
Throw it in the street?

Um-huh! You talking high and mighty.
Talk on—till you get through.

You ain't gonna be able to say a word
If I land my fist on you.

Police! Police!
Come and get this man!
He's trying to ruin the government
And overturn the land!

Copper's whistle!
Patrol bell!
Arrest.

Precinct Station.
Iron cell.
Headlines in press:

MAN THREATENS LANDLORD

TENANT HELD NO BAIL

JUDGE GIVES NEGRO 90 DAYS IN COUNTY JAIL

Langston Hughes

'NOBODY LOSES ALL THE TIME'

nobody loses all the time

i had an uncle named
Sol who was a born failure and
nearly everybody said he should have gone
into vaudeville perhaps because my Uncle Sol could
sing McCann He Was A Diver on Xmas Eve like Hell Itself which
may or may not account for the fact that my Uncle

Sol indulged in that possibly most inexcusible
of all to use a highfalootin phrase
luxuries that is or to
wit farming and be
it needlessly
added

my Uncle Sol's farm
failed because the chickens
ate the vegetables so
my Uncle Sol had a
chicken farm till the
skunks ate the chickens when

my Uncle Sol
had a skunk farm but
the skunks caught cold and
died and so
my Uncle Sol imitated the
skunks in a subtle manner

or by drowning himself in the watertank
but somebody who'd given my Uncle Sol a Victor
Victrola and records while he lived presented to
him upon the auspicious occasion of his decease a
scrumptious not to mention splendiferous funeral with
tall boys in black gloves and flowers and everything and

i remember we all cried like the Missouri
when my Uncle Sol's coffin lurched because
somebody pressed a button
(and down went
my Uncle
Sol

and started a worm farm)

E. E. Cummings

THE CURATE'S KINDNESS

A WORKHOUSE IRONY

I

I thought they'd be strangers aroun' me,
  But she's to be there!
Let me jump out o' waggon and go back and drown me
  At Pummery or Ten-Hatches Weir.

II

I thought: Well, I've come to the Union—
  The workhouse at last—
After honest hard work all the week, and Communion
  O' Zundays, these fifty years past.

III

''Tis hard; but,' I thought, 'never mind it:
  There's gain in the end:
And when I get used to the place I shall find it
  A home, and may find there a friend.

IV

'Life there will be better than t'other,
  For peace is assured.
The men in one wing and their wives in another
  Is strictly the rule of the Board.'

V

Just then one young Pa'son arriving
  Steps up out of breath
To the side o' the waggon wherein we were driving
  To Union; and calls out and saith:

VI

'Old folks, that harsh order is altered,
  Be not sick of heart!
The Guardians they poohed and they pished and they paltered
  When urged not to keep you apart.

' "It is wrong," I maintained, "to divide them,
  Nearly forty years wed."
"Very well, sir. We promise, then, they shall abide them
  In one wing together," they said.'

VIII

Then I sank—knew 'twas quite a foredone thing
  That misery should be
To the end! . . . To get freed of her there was the one thing
  Had made the change welcome to me.

IX

To go there was ending but badly;
  'Twas shame and 'twas pain;

'But anyhow,' thought I, 'thereby I shall gladly
  Get free of this forty years' chain.'

X

I thought they'd be strangers aroun' me,
  But she's to be there!
Let me jump out o' waggon and go back and drown me
  At Pummery or Ten-Hatches Weir.

Thomas Hardy

A MERMAIDEN

CAST UP ON THE CORNISH COAST (AS REPORTED), SEPT. 1934

Chilled with salt dew, tossed on dark waters deep,
Sailors and fishers loved her in their sleep,
And not a few would wed her in their dreams!
  Yet when, within their net, one autumn night
They felt and dragged her sliding weight, it seems
Star-sprinkled skies amid phosphorescent light
On all the billows' tops, and on the net
Making a spider's mesh of sparkles bright,
Dripping like pearls off her curled horse-tail hair—
Low-breathed they haul, and dunch! she's on the planks all right.
What may be done with her can no man fathom, yet
Pretty as paint she starts, but tails so awkwardly.
Nor any of the crew will wish or dare
To take her home and, for their very lives,
To face again their daughters and their wives.

  No fishing clouts will fit her quite, and all in vain
They put her out fried mackerel and hot tea.
Says one, 'Things being at turn of the year
'We'll take ashore the maid, and at the church
'Of Lanteglos-by-Fowey, being near—
'Along with pilchards, breams, and perch,
'Fruit, turnips, autumn-flowers, and marrow,
'Which ornament the choir-stalls, piers, and rails
'And openings of pulpit narrow,
'Put her in window for the Harvest Show!'
  '—Though folk will have to mind her dripping tails
'Upon their bonnets, hymn-books, shawls, and pews.

'I'll hurry to the rector with the news,
'And just remark, "Look here, sir, what we've found!
' "Are we to drop her back, or in a tank
' "Send her along to the Aquarium?" '
'O-ho!' some others cried,
'We'll run her up the High-Street in a barrow.'

An elder stroked his chin, and drank some rum
From wickered bottle: 'Nay, for did we so,
'Being a witch, she'd visit us with woe;
'Or nightmares foul, or other sort of itch—
'She or some kindred doubtful spirit dumb!
'—She weeps, and calls her lover, but in vain,
'These sea-maids marry none but sailors drowned,
'Fetch wind-spouts, or bring whirlpools in calm!'
With this, he smites one crab-fist down in palm,
'I'll just say what, we'll simply scrag the witch!
'And in the cauldron used for melting pitch
'Boil down the tail-end: she is every sailor's foe
'And simply lures poor duffers to their fate.
'The rest we'll cut in lumps and use for bait.'
On this, the boatswain rather sternly spoke:
'Friend, what you say goes farther than a joke.
''Twas honest counsel beyond any doubt,
'Yet did the parish constable find out,
'He and the clergyman would call it guilt:
'So might for her cold blood thy hot be spilt!'

So then a more religious gave his mind:
''Twould be temptation to the village boys
'And frighten half the maids, if they should find
'That ladies such as this should be,
'Who may betroth the dead, or with a spirit
'Vex us, and what our children may inherit:
'And bring about, perhaps, our total loss.
'We, being Christians, needs must sink her with the cross.'

And so with spars and ropes they made her fast
And with the anchor sank. There, fathoms deep,
She found the sandy bottom, so for aye to sleep.

Later near by they hung a passing bell
Hard by a charted rock: which tolls the rising swell.

Thomas Hennell

WELSH INCIDENT

'But that was nothing to what things came out
From the sea-caves of Criccieth yonder.'
'What were they? Mermaids? dragons? ghosts?'
'Nothing at all of any things like that.'
'What were they, then?'
'All sorts of queer things,
Things never seen or heard or written about,
Very strange, un-Welsh, utterly peculiar
Things. Oh, solid enough they seemed to touch,
Had anyone dared it. Marvellous creation,
All various shapes and sizes and no sizes,
All new, each perfectly unlike his neighbour
Though all came moving slowly out together.'
'Describe just one of them.'
'I am unable.'
'What were their colours?'
'Mostly nameless colours,
Colours you'd like to see; but one was puce
Or perhaps more like crimson, but not purplish.
Some had no colour.'
'Tell me, had they legs?'
'Not a leg or foot among them that I saw.'
'But did these things come out in any order?
What o'clock was it? What was the day of the week?
Who else was present? What was the weather?'
'I was coming to that. It was half-past three
On Easter Tuesday last. The sun was shining.
The Harlech Silver Band played *Marchog Jesu*
On thirty-seven shimmering instruments,
Collecting for Caernarvon's (Fever) Hospital Fund.
The populations of Pwllheli, Criccieth,
Portmadoc, Borth, Tremadoc, Penrhyndeudraeth,
Were all assembled. Criccieth's mayor addressed them
First in good Welsh and then in fluent English,
Twisting his fingers in his chain of office,
Welcoming the things. They came out on the sand,
Not keeping time to the band, moving seaward
Silently at a snail's pace. But at last
The most odd, indescribable thing of all
Which hardly one man there could see for wonder
Did something recognizably a some thing.'
'Well, what?'

'It made a noise.'
'A frightening noise?'
'No, no.'
'A musical noise? A noise of scuffling?'
'No, but a very loud, respectable noise—
Like groaning to oneself on Sunday morning
In Chapel, close before the second psalm.'
'What did the mayor do?'
'I was coming to that.'

Robert Graves

YOU'D BETTER BELIEVE HIM

A FABLE

Discovered an old rocking-horse in Woolworth's.
He tried to feed it but without much luck
So he stroked it, had a long conversation about
The trees it came from, the attics it had visited.
Tried to take it out then
But the store detective he
Called the store manager who
Called the police who in court next morning said
'He acted strangely when arrested,
His statement read simply "I believe in rocking-horses".
We have reason to believe him mad.'
'Quite so,' said the prosecution,
'Bring in the rocking-horse as evidence.'
'I'm afraid it's escaped, sir,' said the store manager,
'Left a hoof-print as evidence
On the skull of the store detective.'
'Quite so,' said the prosecution, fearful
of the neighing
Out in the corridor.

Brian Patten

INTERRUPTION AT THE OPERA HOUSE

At the very beginning of an important symphony
while the rich and famous were settling into their quietly
expensive boxes

a man came crashing through the crowds
carrying in his hands a cage in which
the rightful owner of the music sat
yellow and tiny and very poor;
and taking onto the rostrum this rather timid bird
he turned up the microphones, and it sang.

'A very original beginning to the evening' said the crowds
quietly glancing at their programmes to find
the significance of the intrusion.

Meanwhile at the box-office, the organizers of the evening
were arranging for small and uniformed attendants
to evict, even forcefully, the intruders.
But as the attendants, poor and gathered from the nearby
slums at little expense
went rushing down the aisles to do their menial job
they heard above the coughing and irritable rattling of jewels,
a sound that filled their heads with light,
and from somewhere inside them there bubbled up a stream,
and there came a breeze on which their youth was carried.
How sweetly the bird sang!

And though soon the furwrapped crowds
were leaving their boxes and in confusion were winding
their way homeward
still the attendants sat in the aisles,
and some, so delighted at what they heard, rushed out to call
their families and friends.

And their children came
sleepy for it was late in the evening,
very late in the evening,
and they all sat listening
to the rightful owner of the music.

In all the tenement blocks
the lights were clicking on
and the rightful owner of the music
tiny and no longer timid sang
for the rightful owners of the song.

Brian Patten

BIRKETT'S EAGLE

Adam Birkett took his gun
   And climbed from Wasdale Head;
He swore he could spare no more lambs
   To keep an eagle fed.

So Birkett went along the Trod
   That climbs by Gavel Neese,
Till on his right stood Gavel Crag,
   And leftward fell the screes.

The mist whirled up from Ennerdale,
   And Gavel Crag grew dim,
And from the rocks on Birkett's right
   The eagle spoke to him.

'What ails you, Adam Birkett;
   That you have climbed so far
To make an end of Lucifer,
   That was the morning star?

'If there's a heaven, Birkett,
   There's certainly a hell;
And he who would kill Lucifer
   Destroys himself as well.'

The mist whirled off from Gavel Crag,
   And swept towards Beck Head,
And Adam Birkett took his aim
   And shot the eagle dead.

He looked down into Ennerdale
   To where its body fell,
And at his back stood Gavel Crag,
   And at his feet lay Hell.

Birkett scrambled off the rocks,
   And back onto the Trod,
And on his right lay Ennerdale,
   And on his left stood God.

'What was it, Adam Birkett,
   That fell onto the scree?

For I feared it might be Lucifer,
  That once was dear to me.

'And from Carlisle to Ravenglass,
  From Shap to St Bees Head,
There's nobody worth vanquishing
  If Lucifer is dead.'

Birkett's dogs leapt all about
  As he came down the scree,
But he said 'I have killed Lucifer,
  And what is left for me?'

Birkett's lambs leapt all about
  As he came off the fell,
But he said 'I have killed Lucifer,
  And I am dead as well.'

But Lucifer the Morning Star
  Walked thoughtfully away
From the screes beyond the Gavel
  Where the eagle's body lay.

And as he went by Black Sail Pass
  And round below Kirk Fell,
He looked like young Tom Ritson
  Who knew the Birketts well.

And he came down to Wasdale Head,
  Young Ritson to the life,
With an apple in his pocket
  Which he gave to Birkett's wife.

Dorothy S. Howard

BALLAD OF THE BREAD MAN

Mary stood in the kitchen
Baking a loaf of bread,
An angel flew in through the window.
We've a job for you, he said.

God in his big gold heaven,
Sitting in his big blue chair,
Wanted a mother for his little son.
Suddenly saw you there.

Mary shook and trembled,
It isn't true what you say.
Don't say that, said the angel.
The baby's on its way.

Joseph was in the workshop
Planing a piece of wood.
The old man's past it, the neighbours said.
That girl's been up to no good.

And who was that elegant fellow,
They said, in the shiny gear?
The things they said about Gabriel
Were hardly fit to hear.

Mary never answered,
Mary never replied.
She kept the information,
Like the baby, safe inside.

It was election winter.
They went to vote in town.
When Mary found her time had come
The hotels let her down.

The baby was born in an annex
Next to the local pub.
At midnight, a delegation
Turned up from the Farmers' Club.

They talked about an explosion
That made a hole in the sky,
Said they'd been sent to the Lamb & Flag
To see God come down from on high.

A few days later a bishop
And a five-star general were seen
With the head of an African country
In a bullet-proof limousine.

We've come, they said, with tokens
For the little boy to choose.
Told the tale about war and peace
In the television news.

After them came the soldiers
With rifle and bomb and gun,
Looking for enemies of the state.
The family had packed and gone.

When they got back to the village
The neighbours said, to a man,
That boy will never be one of us,
Though he does what he blessed well can.

He went round to all the people
A paper crown on his head.
Here is some bread from my father.
Take, eat, he said.

Nobody seemed very hungry.
Nobody seemed to care.
Nobody saw the god in himself
Quietly standing there.

He finished up in the papers.
He came to a very bad end.
He was charged with bringing the living to life.
No man was that prisoner's friend.

There's only one kind of punishment
To fit that kind of a crime.
They rigged a trial and shot him dead.
They were only just in time.

They lifted the young man by the leg,
They lifted him by the arm,
They locked him in a cathedral
In case he came to harm.

They stored him safe as water
Under seven rocks.
One Sunday morning he burst out
Like a jack-in-the-box.

Through the town he went walking.
He showed them the holes in his head.
Now do you want any loaves? he cried.
Not today, they said.

Charles Causley

PLAINT OF THE OLD MAGICIAN

Carpenter's son, hewer of wood,
I knew him well, well I should.

Carpenter's son, thought he was smart,
Fancied his style in the magic art.

Went to a wedding, switched the wine
To please his Mum, pleased her fine.

Took from a fish a silver coin,
Flashy piece of legerdemain.

Then the bit with fishes and loaves,
He had a lot more up his sleeves.

Martha, Mary—he took them in,
Always fooled single women.

Even persuaded Lazarus
To act a while as his accomplice.

All that claim to heal the sick,
Nothing but a mountebank trick.

Why on earth make such a furor
About an obvious conjuror?

They said he stopped a rising wave,
He said he'd come back from the grave!

They said he was the promised Christ,
I'd say he was an illusionist.

Most of his stunts you can understand
If you know a little sleight-of-hand.

But his final act puzzles me still
For nobody helped him there on the hill.

Carpenter's son, hewer of wood,
They nailed him and they nailed him good.
Some said Hooray,
Some said Shame,
Most that he'd only himself to blame.
In a hole, in a sack,
They put him below
Then blocked the way
And sealed the crack.

Two nights and a day
Then out he came
With a split and a clack!
How he did it I'll never know,
And he'll never go back.
He's here to stay, here to stay.

A. L. Hendriks

PETER AND JOHN

Twelve good friends
Walked under the leaves,
Binding the ends
Of the barley sheaves.

Peter and John
Lay down to sleep
Pillowed upon
A haymaker's heap.

John and Peter
Lay down to dream.
The air was sweeter
Than honey and cream.

Peter was bred
In the salty cold:
His hair was red
And his eyes were gold.

John had a mouth
Like a wing bent down:
His brow was smooth
And his eyes were brown.

Peter to slumber
Sank like a stone,
Of all their number
The bravest one.

John more slowly
Composed himself,
Young and holy
Among the Twelve.

John as he slept
Cried out in grief,
Turned and wept
On the golden leaf:

'Peter, Peter,
Stretch me your hand
Across the glitter
Of the harvest land!

'Peter, Peter,
Give me a sign!
This was a bitter
Dream of mine—

'Bitter as aloes
It parched my tongue.
Upon the gallows
My life was hung.

'Sharp it seemed
As a bloody sword.
Peter, I dreamed
I was Christ the Lord!'

Peter turned
To holy Saint John:
His body burned
In the falling sun.

In the falling sun
He burned like a flame:
'John, Saint John,
I have dreamed the same!

'My bones were hung
On an elder tree;
Bells were rung
Over Galilee.

'A silver penny
Sealed each of my eyes.
Many and many
A cock crew thrice.'

When Peter's word
Was spoken and done,
'Were you Christ the Lord
In your dream?' said John.

'No,' said the other,
'That I was not.
I was our brother
Iscariot.'

Elinor Wylie

LORD OF THE DANCE

I danced in the morning
When the world was begun,
And I danced in the moon
And the stars and the sun
And I came down from heaven
And I danced on the earth—
At Bethlehem I had my birth.

Dance then wherever you may be;
I am the Lord of the Dance, said he,
I'll lead you all, wherever you may be,
I will lead you all in the Dance, said he.

I danced for the scribe
And the pharisee,
But they would not dance
And they couldn't follow me;
I danced for the fishermen,
For James and John—
They came with me
And the dance went on.

I danced on the Sabbath
And I cured the lame;
The holy people
Said it was a shame;
They whipped and they stripped
And they hung me high,
And they left me there
On a Cross to die.

I danced on a Friday
When the sky turned black—
It's hard to dance
With the devil on your back;
They buried my body
And they thought I'd gone—
But I am the dance
And I still go on.

They cut me down
And I leapt up high—
I am the life
That'll never, never die;
I'll live in you
If you'll live in me—
I am the Lord
Of the Dance, said he.

Dance then wherever you may be;
I am the Lord of the Dance, said he,
I'll lead you all, wherever you may be,
I will lead you all in the Dance, said he.

Sydney Carter

Index of Poets

Alphabetical index of poets with titles of poems

Sources and Acknowledgements

Thanks are due to the authors (or their executors), their representatives and publishers mentioned in the following list for their kind permission to reproduce copyright material:

W. H. Auden: 'O What Is That Sound?' from *Collected Poems* (Faber and Faber).
Michael Baldwin: 'My Friend Tom' from *How Charles Egget Lost His Way in a Creation Myth* (Secker and Warburg).
Patricia Beer: 'Abbey Tomb' from *Just Like the Resurrection* (Macmillan).
Roy Bennett: 'Mr Gedge'.
Elizabeth Bishop: 'The Fish' from *The Complete Poems* (Farrar, Straus & Giroux Inc.).
Gwendolyn Brooks: 'Sadie and Maud' from *The World of Gwendolyn Brooks,* © Gwendolyn Brooks Blakely. Reprinted by permission of Harper & Row.
George Mackay Brown: 'The Hawk' from *The Year of the Whale* (Hogarth Press).
David Campbell: 'Men in Green' from *Selected Poems* (Angus and Robertson).
Sydney Carter: 'Lord of the Dance' (Stainer and Bell).
Charles Causley: 'Ballad of the Bread Man', 'If You Should Go to Caistor Town', 'Lord Lovelace', 'Miller's End', 'The Ballad of Charlotte Dymond' from *Collected Poems* (Macmillan); 'Nelson Gardens' from *Figure of Eight* (Macmillan).
Leonard Clark: 'The Goole Captain'.
R. P. Tristram Coffin: 'Little Boys of Texas' from *Collected Poems* (Macmillan Publishing Co. Inc.).
E. E. Cummings: 'anyone lived in a pretty how town', 'nobody loses all the time' from *The Complete Poems of E. E. Cummings* (Granada Publishing Ltd).
Clifford Dyment: 'The Desert' from *Collected Poems* (J. M. Dent).
Donald Finkel: 'Hunting Song' from *The Clothing's New Emperor.*
Robert Graves: 'Welsh Incident' from *Collected Poems* (Cassell).
A. L. Hendriks: 'Plaint of the Old Magician' (Outposts).
Thomas Hennell: 'A Mermaiden' from *Lady Filmy Fern* (Hamish Hamilton).
A. E. Housman: 'Bredon Hill' from *Collected Poems* (Jonathan Cape) by permission of The Society of Authors as the literary representative of the Estate of A. E. Housman.
Dorothy S. Howard: 'Birkett's Eagle'.

Langston Hughes: 'Ballad of the Landlord' from *Montage of a Dream Deferred* (Henry Holt). Reprinted by permission of Harold Ober Associates Inc. Copyright ©1949 by Curtis Publishing Co. Renewed 1976.
Ted Hughes: 'Pike' from *Lupercal* (Faber and Faber).
Ada Jackson: 'Church School' and 'Our Brother Richard'.
Henry Herbert Knibbs: 'Charley Lee' from *Songs of the Lost Frontier* (Houghton Mifflin Co.).
Philip Larkin: 'The Explosion' from *High Windows* (Faber and Faber).
John Lehmann: 'The Ballad of Banners (1944)' from *The Age of the Dragon* (Longman Group).
Laurence Lerner: 'The Day We Found the Snow Palace'.
C. Day Lewis: 'The Unexploded Bomb' from *The Gate* (Jonathan Cape) by permission of the Executors of the Estate of C. Day Lewis.
Nigel Lewis: 'A Cautionary Tale'.
Douglas Livingstone: 'Sunstrike' from *Sjambok and Other Poems* (Oxford University Press).
F. L. Lucas: 'Spain, 1809' from *From Many Times and Lands* (The Bodley Head).
George MacBeth: 'Bedtime Story' from *The Broken Places.*
John Manifold: 'The Griesly Wife'.
John Masefield: 'Reynard the Fox' (extracts) by permission of The Society of Authors as the literary representative of the Estate of John Masefield.
Edgar Lee Masters: ' "Butch" Weldy' from *Spoon River Anthology.* Reprinted by permission of T. Werner Laurie at The Bodley Head.
W. S. Merwin: 'Ballad of John Cable and Three Gentlemen' from *A Mask for Janus* (Yale University Press).
Ernest G. Moll: 'Sheep Killer' from Poems 1940-1955 (Angus and Robertson (UK) Ltd).
Leslie Norris: 'The Ballad of Billy Rose' from *Finding Gold* (Chatto and Windus).
Brian Patten: 'Interruption at the Opera House' from *The Irrelevant Song* (Allen & Unwin); 'You'd Better Believe Him' from *Notes to the Hurrying Man* (Allen & Unwin).
Margaret Rhodes: 'Souvenirs'.
Louis Simpson: 'Carentan O Carentan' from *A Dream of Governors* (Wesleyan University Press).
Stevie Smith: 'The Parklands' from *Collected Poems* (Allen Lane) by permission of James MacGibbon.
Wole Soyinka: 'Telephone Conversation'.
L. A. G. Strong: 'Coroner's Jury' from *The Body's Imperfection* (Collins).
Wilfred Watson: 'The Juniper Tree' from *Friday's Child* (Faber and Faber).
Harri Webb: 'A True Story' from *A Crown for Bronwen* (J. D. Lewis & Sons, Gomer Press).
David Wevill: 'The Birth of a Shark' from *The Birth of a Shark* (Macmillan).
Elinor Wylie: 'Peter and John' from *Collected Poems of Elinor Wylie.* Copyright 1928 by Alfred A. Knopf, Inc., and renewed 1956 by Edwina C. Rubenstein. Reprinted by permission of Alfred A Knopf, Inc.